THE BOOK OF
FIVE RINGS

MIYAMOTO MUSASHI

Translation by
William Scott Wilson

Calligraphy by
Shiro Tsujimura

KODANSHA INTERNATIONAL
Tokyo · New York · London

NOTE

Throughout this volume, Japanese names appear
in the traditional order,
surname preceding given name

Shrike on a Withered Branch (page 8) copyright ©
Kuboso Memorial Museum of Arts, Izumi.
The portrait of Miyamoto Musashi (page 70) copyright ©
Shimada Museum of Art.

Distributed in the United States by Kodansha America, Inc.,
and in the United Kingdom and continental Europe
by Kodansha Europe Ltd.

Published by Kodansha International Ltd.,
17–14 Otowa 1-chome, Bunkyo-ku, Tokyo 112–8652.

Translation copyright © 2002 William Scott Wilson
and Kodansha International Ltd.
All rights reserved. Printed in Japan.
ISBN 978-4-7700-2801-3

First Edition, 2002
08 09 10 11 12 13 14 15   20 19 18 17 16 15 14

www.kodansha-intl.com

The English translation is dedicated to
Sifu Steve Williams

CONTENTS

THE BOOK OF FIVE RINGS

Shrike on a Withered Branch by Miyamoto Musashi

FOREWORD

In a private collection in Japan, there is a remarkable painting, nearly four hundred years old, of a shrike on a withered branch. Done in monochrome India ink and measuring about four feet high by a foot and a half wide, it expresses a tension and clarity of spirit that seem to go far beyond the bounds of its relatively few lines. The shrike sits with extraordinary attention and concentration, its sharp beak a subtle and almost cruel curve, its gaze cast into the void. It is clearly a bird such as we rarely see in our back yards. As we continue to look at this work, it is the single stroke depicting the greater part of the branch that becomes most arresting. Rising up from the bottom left of the painting and cutting through its near center, it is grace and strength in a single quick movement, standing out against nothingness; the observer might conclude that the painter must have been, in a sense, absolutely fearless. How else the decisiveness and total self-confidence of this one swordlike stroke?

The painter's name was Niten, or "Two Heavens." More exactly, Niten was the artistic name of one Shinmen Musashi, or Miyamoto Musashi.

With the publication of *The Book of Five Rings*, I feel a sense of completion on what might be considered a short cycle of translations of works centering around Japanese warrior thought and concerns. Musashi, who was the ultimate combatant on the field, reveals his techniques for defeating one's opponent through spirit, awareness and discipline. For him, the only goal is victory: there is no other point to combat, whether in one-on-one confrontations or on the battlefield for his lord. What is gained along the Way of this discipline, however, is a grasp of all the other arts, both martial and literary. In *The Unfettered Mind*, the Zen priest Takuan, a contemporary of Musashi, teaches the defeat of the interfering ego—the overriding sense of self, over which we often stumble—specifically in its first essay, "The Mysterious Record of Immovable Wisdom." Writing to one of the sword masters to the shogun, Takuan uses the example of martial combat to explain the Zen approach to handling the ego, and so deals with the transcendental area including both life and death.

In the third work of this cycle, the *Hagakure*, Yamamoto Tsunetomo considers the warrior values of loyalty, duty and righteousness, and finds his ultimate realization of these matters in death. To Tsunetomo, a man's death demonstrated his sincerity, and in considering himself as already dead, he was able to complete his daily work with utter peace and tranquility. Musashi, Takuan and Tsunetomo, it would seem, are concerned with the elimination of fear, and how to engage in life in a straightforward and unwavering manner. It is Musashi, however, who deals with the subject with an astonishing practicality and realism, and he encourages us to cut through any obstacles with energy and self-reliance. Asking no aid from the gods and Buddhas, we brace ourselves only with an internalized Way.

Musashi wrote *The Book of Five Rings* toward the very end of his life, after fighting in over sixty individual matches and at least three major battles on the field. That we have such easy access to his reflections on his life-and-death experiences should, I think, be both congratulatory and an admonishment, for it grants us the ability to be conversant with the wisdom learned from intense experiences that very few of us will ever have, and may show us how lightly we take our own lives and potential. Accordingly, while *The Book of Five Rings* will be of extraordinary interest to practitioners of the martial arts and students of Japanese culture, its study will be of value for anyone whose life encompasses conflict.

Musashi's original manuscript of five scrolls no longer exists, but the various copies made differ only slightly in some of the words and phrases. Remarkably, the copy presented by Musashi's disciple Terao Nobumasa to Yamamoto Gensuke, in 1667 (only twenty years after Musashi's death), is still in the possession of the Hosokawa family, whose ancestor, the daimyo Hosokawa Tadatoshi, was Musashi's primary benefactor. It is considered to be the most accurate of those extant, and it is the copy upon which this translation is based.

Finally, I would like to express my gratitude to the following people: Mr. Kuramochi Tetsuo, Senior Executive Editor at Kodansha International, for kindly suggesting and coordinating this project; Professor Matsumoto Michihiro, who wrote the modern Japanese translation accompanying the bilingual version of this publication; Messrs. Kamata Shigeo and Watanabe Ichiro for their clear notes and translations of the original into modern Japanese, from which I benefited greatly; Ms. Emily David for her encouragement and patience in listening to me talk about little else for a period of many months; and my late professors, Hiraga Noburu and Richard McKinnon, whom I still feel looking over my shoulder with friendly bemusement. Any and all mistakes are my own.

William Scott Wilson
October 10, 2000

INTRODUCTION

We have very few reliable facts about Musashi's life. His own words on the subject fill less than a page at the beginning of *The Book of Five Rings*, and later accounts such as the *Nitenki* or the *Tanba Hokin Hikki* were all written eighty to one hundred and thirty years after his death. However, a bare-bones biography might be pieced together, with events that are commonly accepted as true from the sources that are available. These include a memorial inscription of stone erected nine years after Musashi's death by his adopted son and the priest with whom the swordsman studied Zen Buddhism in his later years, plus what was noted of his comings and goings by the Hosokawa clan in northern Kyushu. We must exclude legendary feats of speed and skill attributed to Musashi since they are at once unreliable and go against the spirit of Musashi's writings. Those interested in the full gamut of stories that grew up around Musashi's life should read *Musashi*, the endlessly entertaining historical fiction written by Yoshikawa Eiji, or see the film *Samurai Trilogy*, directed by Inagaki Hiroshi.

MUSASHI

In *The Book of Five Rings*, Musashi notes that he was born in Harima, but there is also evidence that he came from the village of Miyamoto, in Mimasaka.[1] Neither claim can be proven. The date of his birth is unclear, but according to his own account, he was born in 1584. His father, Shinmen Munisai, was said to be a master of the *jitte* (a small metal club with an extended "thumb" for countering a sword), and may have left the family when Musashi was quite young.

When Musashi was thirteen, he fought and defeated a swordsman of the Shinto Style, Arima Kihei, in Harima. His second match and subsequent victory was at the age of sixteen, when he defeated a martial artist from Tajima by the name of Akiyama. It is said that he joined the Toyotomi forces (which lost) at the historically decisive Battle of Sekigahara in 1600, but this, too, is uncertain. The next few years must have been spent in hard training, for at the age of twenty-one Musashi went to Kyoto and fought a series of engagements with the Yoshioka clan, which held the position of martial arts instructor to the shogun's family in that city. After maiming the eldest brother, Yoshioka Seijuro, with a wooden sword and killing the second brother, Denshichiro, Musashi fought off a group of Yoshioka disciples who, beneath the pines of the Ichijo temple, tried but failed to take revenge. It is said that it was during the fight with Seijuro that Musashi's eyes were opened to the "Two Heavens," or Two-Sword Style.

Leaving the Yoshiokas in disarray, Musashi met and defeated a disciple of the famous In'ei, a spearman-priest at the Hozoin. Traveling to Edo, he then fought Muso Gonnosuke, the famous staff martial artist, in the only contest that may have been considered a draw. A little later he fought and defeated a practitioner of the Yagyu Style, a style that would become one of the most famous of the period. Moving on to Iga, he met with the well-known sickle-and-chain martial artist, Shishido Baikin, and defeated him as well.

In April of 1612, Musashi left Kyoto and went to Kokura in northern Kyushu. There he sought out one of his father's former disciples, now a senior official of the Kokura fief, in order to gain permission to have a match with Ganryu Sasaki Kojiro. Kojiro was employed as a sword teacher to the Hosokawa clan and was famous for his long "Drying Pole" sword and Swallow Style. This famous match was held on Funashima, now called Ganryushima, a small lonely island in the sea off Kokura. Tradition has it that as Musashi was being rowed to the island, he carved a wooden sword from an extra oar, and it was with this "sword" that he quickly brained his unfortunate opponent. Kojiro did not survive the blow.

According to some accounts, Musashi next surfaced in 1615 to take part in the military action at Osaka Castle, the final fall of the Toyotomi clan. After that he seems to have set out through the northern provinces of Dewa and Hitachi, where he may have taken on his disciple, Iori, who was later to become his adopted son. He then returned to Nagoya in Owari and toured a number of other provinces, always seeking out matches with other martial artists.

In 1634, Musashi travelled again to Kokura, now under the authority of Ogasawara Tadazane, and stayed a number of years. In 1637, he seems to have participated in the attack on Hara Castle during the Shimabara Rebellion, in which he received several wounds. Having returned to Kyoto for recuperation, he is said to have met Hosokawa Tadatoshi, the master of Kumamoto Castle, at a literary group in 1640, and to have been invited by the latter to stay as a guest with his own residence in the castle town. Musashi accepted and continued to practice and teach his martial art there.

In February of 1641, at the request of Lord Hosokawa, Musashi wrote down the *Thirty-five Articles of the Martial Arts* (兵法三十五箇条). This was the first time he recorded his own style in writing, and it was from this document in outline form that he eventually would write *The Book of Five Rings*. Tragically, Tadatoshi passed away shortly afterward at the age of fifty-four, dashing Musashi's hopes for an official endorsement of his style. Thus began a period when the famous swordsman concentrated increasingly on poetry, tea, painting and sculpture.

By 1643, Musashi must have felt the intimations of what was to be a fatal disease. On October 10 of that year, in an act of purification, he "climbed Mount Iwato in the province of Higo on the island of Kyushu, bowed in veneration to Heaven, worshipped Kannon and stood before the Buddha," and began to compose *The Book of Five Rings*. This he would complete after two years of meditation on his experiences.

Around the springtime of 1645, his disease, which is thought to have been some form of thoracic cancer, gradually worsened, and in April he retreated to the Reigan Cave on Mount Iwato (also called Mount Iwatono), where he had practiced zazen during previous years, and where he wanted to wait peacefully for death. However, he was convinced to return to his residence, where he could be looked after by his disciples. On May 12, his disease becoming critical, Musashi gave out parting gifts to his disciples. His final act was to write out "The Way of Walking Alone" (or "The Way of Self-Reliance"; 独行道), twenty-one points on self-discipline for later generations.

On May 19, 1645, Miyamoto (Shinmen) Musashi died at his residence, by most accounts, at the age of sixty-two. A requiem was given soon after by the priest Shunzan, with whom Musashi had studied Zen. As the priest intoned the sutras, it is said that the sky suddenly clouded over and there was an enormous clap of thunder. Thus was it known that the great swordsman had passed away.

THE KYOTO RENAISSANCE

"I have never had a teacher while studying the Ways of the various arts and accomplishments, or in anything at all" ("The Earth Chapter").

This is an astonishing statement from a man who was not only one of the most famous swordsmen of his time, but also an extraordinarily skilled painter, sculptor and metallurgist. We also know that Musashi was well acquainted with poetry, the Way of Tea, the recitation of Noh drama and perhaps even carpentry. This necessitates an adjustment of the picture we may have of him as a man of strength and skill (both qualities he would regard as of secondary importance) who did little other than wander the country engaging other martial artists in matches he inevitably won. In order to make that adjustment, we must consider the world in which he lived and the people with whom he may have been in contact.

Musashi was active during a time aptly called the Kyoto Renaissance, a period stretching approximately fifty years on either side of the year 1600. After suffering a devastating century and a half of civil wars during which countless art treasures were destroyed, ancient temples and buildings burned, and libraries lost forever, Japan was brought back to unification and eventual peace by the efforts of three successive warlords: Oda Nobunaga (1534–82), Toyotomi Hideyoshi (1536–98) and Tokugawa Ieyasu (1542–1616). After so many years of social disruption, the response to this peace was a surge in economic prosperity and a concomitant flourishing of the arts in almost every arena. Castle architecture blossomed, there was a new interest in classical poetry and painting, the art of the tea ceremony reached its height, the world of ceramics spread in new directions, and schools in the martial arts proliferated, with every new disciple striking out on his own. How the various players of this period influenced Musashi is not documented, but considering his artistic talent and curiosity, his insistence that we know all the arts, and the time he spent in Kyoto, it is germane, I think, to look briefly at two men representative of the period with whom he is likely to have associated.

At the aesthetic center of the Kyoto Renaissance was Hon'ami Koetsu (1558–1637), a man whom tradition, if not recorded evidence, links with Musashi. Koetsu came from a family of sword polishers and appraisers—well known in that field since the fourteenth century—and was much in demand for his skills in this work. Still, there were very few other arts that he did not practice. Granted by the shogun an area of land—Takagamine, or Takaramine—just outside of Kyoto, he established an art colony that would act as a sort of launching pad for everything from paper making to lacquerware to pottery. Koetsu himself is best known today for his calligraphy and pottery, but his strong ties to the samurai sword and his intense and friendly personality must have made him a congenial sometime companion for the lone martial artist. Koetsu's strong interest in Noh recitation may have sparked Musashi's later participation in that art as well. One of Koetsu's friends, Sakon Daiyu, was the head of the Kanze school of Noh, and it is not unlikely that Musashi would have made his acquaintance along with many others in the arts. Among Koetsu's other associates were Tawaraya Sotatsu, the painter; Furuta Oribe, the warrior and tea master; Raku Don'yu, the potter to the tea masters; and Hayashi Razan, the Confucian scholar. Musashi could not have helped being influenced by this society of talented men, even if only peripherally, and Koetsu's reputed strong character and intense dislike of greed would have fit well with the same tendencies in the swordsman's personality.

Musashi insisted that through an intense study and practice of the Way of the Martial Arts, the Ways of all other arts would be understood. That his acquaintance with the older sword-polisher-turned-aesthete may have helped open his eyes to this understanding is not recorded, but the jovial shadow of Hon'ami Koetsu seems indeed to pass over the pages of *The Book of Five Rings*.

Takuan Soho (1573–1645), a Zen Buddhist priest of the Rin-zai sect, was another influential character of the Kyoto Renaissance traditionally connected to Musashi. Like Koetsu, Takuan was a polymath who excelled in calligraphy, painting, poetry, gardening and the tea ceremony. He must have also enjoyed being in the kitchen, for he invented the pickle still used as a constant in the Japanese diet and, to this day, it retains his name. Takuan was a prodigious writer whose collected works fill six volumes. He was an advisor to the emperor and shogun alike, and became abbot of the Daitokuji, a major Zen temple in Kyoto, by the age of thirty-five.

The tradition that names Takuan an instructor to Musashi is interesting in a number of ways, but is brought to focus in Takuan's essay "The Mysterious Record of Immovable Wisdom," written not to Musashi, but to Yagyu Munenori, the head of the Shinkage Style of swordsmanship. The work deals in part with the relationship of the mind, body and technique, a subject covered extensively in *The Book of Five Rings*. In the very beginning of his essay, Takuan tells us:

What is called Fudo Myo-o [a wrathful manifestation of the central Buddha Vairocana] is said to be one's unmoving mind and an unvacillating body. Unvacillating means not being detained by anything. Glancing at something and not stopping the mind is called Immovable. This is because when the mind stops at something, the breast is filled with various judgments, and there are various movements within it. When its movements cease, the stopping mind moves, but does not move at all . . . When you first notice the sword that is moving to strike you, if you think of meeting that sword just as it is, your mind will stop at the sword in just that position, your own movements will be undone, and you will be cut down by your opponent . . .

The action of Spark and Stone . . . underscores the point that the mind should not be detained by things; it says that even with speed it is essential that the mind does not stop. When the mind stops, it will be grasped by the opponent. On the other hand, if the mind contemplates being fast and goes into quick action, it will be captured by its own contemplation . . . Putting the mind in one place is called falling into one-sidedness. One-sidedness is said to be bias in one place. Correctness is in moving about anywhere. The Correct Mind shows itself by extending the mind throughout the body. It is not biased in any one place . . . The effort not to stop the mind in just one place—this is discipline. Not stopping the mind is the object and essence. Put nowhere, it will be everywhere. Even in moving the mind outside the body, if it is sent in one direction, it will be lacking in nine others. If the mind is not restricted to just one direction, it will be in all ten.[2]

This is one of the main, mostly implicit themes that runs like a current throughout *The Book of Five Rings*. And while these words in no way exhaust the subject of the relationship between the sword and Zen, they are most certainly at the very center of the subject. One can imagine Musashi listening quietly and drinking them in like pure water.

Musashi's association with the artists and Buddhist priests of the Kyoto Renaissance cannot be accurately documented but, at the same time, in no way can it be dismissed. It is clear that in terms of his own development from rural birth to being both an undefeated swordsman and talented multiple artist, he would have had, if not teachers, then companions and associates on the Way. Kyoto is and always has been a very connected society, with strong relationships among people of high aesthetic abilities. Nor was this social network limited to Kyoto. Even in his wanderings around the country, Musashi may well have encountered eccentric Zen artists (his contemporary Fugai comes to mind) as surely as he encountered the sixty-odd martial artists he would fight and defeat.

Musashi's final domicile, where he taught, meditated and wrote his book, was not Kyoto, but faraway Kumamoto, in northern Kyushu. Yet even this place was the home of the Hosokawa, one of Japan's oldest and most artistic warrior clans. And while his main benefactor there was the daimyo Hosokawa Tadatoshi, he would likely have met and talked with the latter's father, Tadaoki, a master politician, a master in the Way of Tea, a campaigner of every talent and a lacquerware artist beyond compare. We can see Musashi having tea with the old man, the rough hands that held the sword so many times cradling a Chojiro tea bowl, and talking about the Way of the Warrior.

"For those who would study my martial art, there are rules for putting it into practice: . . . Touch upon all of the arts" (from "The Earth Chapter").

BUDDHISM AND *THE BOOK OF FIVE RINGS*

Much has been made of Musashi's Buddhism and, paradoxically, his lack of the same. In the very beginning of *The Book of Five Rings*, he tells us that before starting the book he "bowed in veneration to Heaven, worshipped Kannon[3] and stood before the Buddha."[4] A few lines later he informs us that "in writing this book I am not borrowing the ancient words of Buddhism . . ." And then, "I will express the heart of Truth, using the Ways of Heaven and Kanzeon[5] as mirrors." Accordingly, we can see that Musashi had something of Buddhism in his heart, but he would not try to give his experiences and words legitimacy by invoking Buddhism in his words.

It is clear in *The Book of Five Rings* that the Zen Buddhist insistence on absolute personal experience and transcendence of the interfering self is one of the touchstones of Musashi's thought. We also have the tradition of his relationship with the Zen priest Takuan, and the Hosokawa records of his studying Zen under Abbot Shunzan. But Zen Buddhism was hardly the only religion during Musashi's time. Hon'ami Koetsu came from a long line of Nichiren-sect Buddhists and, indeed, most of the artists at his colony in Takagamine belonged to that sect. Hosokawa Tadaoki's wife, Gracia, was a Japanese Christian, although Tadaoki was not. Then there is the Shingon Buddhist faith, which has run like an undercurrent in Japanese culture since the eighth century, a sect which believes that anything of beauty, in nature or in art, partakes of the Buddha nature. Could Musashi, as a wanderer through the countryside and an artist, have been immune to such ideas?

How much did Musashi's religious convictions or practices influence his martial art? *The Book of Five Rings* gives us only a hint, but it is worthwhile, I think, to look at that hint with a little more focus.

The Five Rings, which is both part of the title and forms the structure of the book, refers to the Buddhist theory of the Five Elements, and Musashi gives only a short statement for the choice of this motif: Earth, because it symbolized his fundamental view of the martial arts; Water, because of his own style based on fluidity and purity; Fire, or battle, because of its energy and ability for quick change; Wind, the other style, because of the double meaning ("wind" and "style") of the Chinese character; and Emptiness, because this is ultimately the place from which all other activities come.

The Five Elements come from a long religious tradition, and are used as objects of meditation in many different ways. Musashi, inquisitive as he was, would have been at least conversant with these.

Besides their traditional characteristics of solidity and hardness (Earth), fluidity (Water), heat and activity (Fire), motion (Wind) and the encompassment of all the other four (Emptiness), the Five Elements have each traditionally been aligned with a direction and a meditation Buddha as well. Thus, Earth contains the direction south and the Buddha Ratnasambhava; Water, the east and the Buddha Akshobya; Fire, the west and the Buddha Amitabha; Wind, or Air, the north and the Buddha Amoghasiddhi; and Emptiness, the center of all directions and the central Buddha Vairocana. Each of these Buddhas has its own meaning, color, symbol and transformational wisdom. In esoteric Buddhism, each of them, along with their respective qualities, is to be meditated on in turn as a method of more effective resolution of life's problems and as a way leading to eventual enlightenment.

Such meanings would have been clear to Musashi and his disciples, but would not necessarily have been spelled out by Musashi in a book on martial arts. The significance of the selection of the Five Elements for both the title and the structure of his work, however, remains.

In passing, it is interesting to note that one of Musashi's most famous sculptures depicts Fudo Myo-o, a wrathful manifestation of the central Buddha Vairocana, who represents the fundamental nature of the universe. This Fudo Myo-o, whose name means "Immovable Wisdom King," is represented with a sword to cut through our ignorance and a rope to bind up our emotions (actions Musashi deemed essential in the martial arts for being more effective). While given a wrathful expression, the figure is moved fundamentally by compassion, the very essence of the Kannon whom Musashi worshipped before writing this book. Both Fudo and Kannon are the symbols of the unshakable tranquillity Musashi sought to translate to his students in their moments of life and death.

Musashi wrote *The Book of Five Rings* at the end of his life as a guidebook for the disciples he had taught face to face. It was a broad outline, in a sense, of work he had done with them over a period of years, a reminder or prompt to guide them after he was gone. Some items were apparently so inimical to the written word that, after a line or two defining the subject, he simply wrote, "This is an oral tradition," meaning that it had to be passed on person to person rather than in a book.

Though the vehicle of this book is technique, its essence is mind. To Musashi, the martial arts were an approach, or psychology, to the Way. They were not something to be bought and sold, as so many of the martial arts schools both then and now make them out to be, nor were they something to decorate one's life. Conflict is real. The Way is real. The student must use his or her real experience to resolve the two. And it is mind, far more than technique, that will be the enabler. Musashi insisted on the importance of real experience, and the reader should not miss the fact that the phrase "You should investigate this thoroughly" is repeated more than any other in the book.

One week before he died, Musashi continued to press his points home. Picking up his brush and, as the Zen masters would say, with the kindness of an old grandmother, he wrote out "The Way of Self-Reliance," or literally, "The Way of Walking Alone" (独行道)—twenty-one items to help the students of the future nail down what was theirs alone. It is fitting to end this short introduction with what would be his last admonition.

THE WAY OF WALKING ALONE

(or *The Way of Self-Reliance*)

- Do not turn your back on the various Ways of this world.

- Do not scheme for physical pleasure.

- Do not intend to rely on anything.

- Consider yourself lightly; consider the world deeply.

- Do not ever think in acquisitive terms.

- Do not regret things about your own personal life.

- Do not envy another's good or evil.

- Do not lament parting on any road whatsoever.

- Do not complain or feel bitterly about yourself or others.

- Have no heart for approaching the path of love.

- Do not have preferences.

- Do not harbor hopes for your own personal home.

- Do not have a liking for delicious food for yourself.

- Do not carry antiques handed down from generation to generation.

- Do not fast so that it affects you physically.

- While it's different with military equipment, do not be fond of material things.

- While on the Way, do not begrudge death.

- Do not be intent on possessing valuables or a fief in old age.

- Respect the gods and Buddhas, but do not depend on them.

- Though you give up your life, do not give up your honor.

- Never depart from the Way of the Martial Arts.

Second Day of the Fifth Month, Second Year of Shoho [1645]
Shinmen Musashi

THE EARTH
CHAPTER

I have named my own Way of the Martial Arts the "Two Heavens, One Style,"[1] and after many years of discipline have thought to describe it in a book for the first time.

In the first week or so of the Tenth Month in the Twentieth Year of Kan'ei [1643], I climbed Mount Iwato in the province of Higo on the island of Kyushu, bowed in veneration to Heaven, worshipped Kannon[2] and stood before the Buddha. Born in the province of Harima, I am the warrior Shinmen Musashi no kami Fujiwara no Genshin. I have now reached the age of sixty.

From long ago in my youth I set my mind on the martial arts, and had my first match when I was thirteen. My opponent was a martial artist of the Shinto Style, Arima Kihei, whom I defeated. At the age of sixteen I defeated a strong martial artist by the name of Tajima no Akiyama. At the age of twenty I went to the capital and met with famous martial artists; and, although I fought a number of matches, I was never unable to take the victory. After that, I went from province to province, from place to place, and encountered martial artists from many different schools; and though I fought as many as sixty matches, I did not lose even once. All of these were events occurring from the time I was thirteen until I reached twenty-eight or twenty-nine.

When I had passed the age of thirty and thought back over my life, I understood that I had not been a victor because of extraordinary skill in the martial arts. Perhaps I had some natural talent or had not departed from natural principles. Or again, was it that the martial arts of the other styles were lacking somewhere?

After that, determined all the more to reach a clearer understanding of the deep principles, I practiced day and night. By about the time I was fifty, I realized the Way of this martial art quite naturally. Since then, I have spent my time without taking the road of exhaustive investigation. Entrusting myself to the principles of my martial art, I have never had a teacher while studying the Ways of the various arts and accomplishments, or in anything at all. Now, even in writing this book, I am neither borrowing the ancient words of Buddhism or Confucianism, nor using old examples from the military chronicles or practices. Within the view of this one style, I will express the heart of Truth, using the Ways of Heaven and Kanzeon as mirrors.

Taking up my brush at one revolution past the Hour of the Tiger [4:30 a.m.], on the night of the tenth day of the Tenth Month, I begin this book.

What is called the "martial art" is the standard of the military clans. Commanders, in particular, should put it into practice, and common soldiers should know its Way as well. Yet there are no warriors who clearly understand the Way of the Martial Arts in the world today.

First, as representatives of Ways, Buddhism is a Way of salvation for man, Confucianism venerates a Way of culture, and medicine is a Way of curing various diseases. Moreover, poets teach the Way of Japanese verse; and then there are tea masters, archers and others who teach the various arts. All of these practice according to their own thoughts and relish what they do according to their own hearts. It is a rare person who relishes the Way of the Martial Arts.

The term "warrior" speaks of the "Two Ways of Culture and Conflict,"[3] and to relish these two is our Way. A warrior should make his best effort in the martial arts according to his own abilities and situation, even if he is naturally untalented in this Way. Generally speaking, when people contemplate the heart of warrior thought, they consider it no better than a way in which being a warrior is simply in dying. But the Way of dying is not limited to warriors alone. For even monks, women, farmers and the classes below them, there is no distinction in their having a sense of duty, in knowing shame and in being resolved to their own deaths. What is most basic in the Way of practicing the martial arts is overcoming your opponent in each and any event, whether in victory over a single opponent in a duel, or in victory in a fight with a number of men. One desires to make a name for himself and to raise his position, whether for his lord's sake or his own. This is accomplished by virtue of the martial arts.

There are many people who, even when studying the Way of the Martial Arts, think that these skills will not be useful in real situations. In fact, the true Way of the Martial Arts is to train so that these skills are useful at any time, and to teach these skills so that they will be useful in all things.

THE WAY OF THE MARTIAL ARTS

In China and even in our own country, those who have put this Way into practice have traditionally been spoken of as masters of the martial arts. As a warrior, one should necessarily study this practice. These days, the men making their way through the world calling themselves martial artists are generally only teachers of sword techniques. Recently, the priests of the Kashima and Kantori shrines in the province of Hitachi have established various styles, declaring them to have been transmitted by the gods, and have traveled from province to province teaching them to others.

Since times past, among the various achievements and arts, there has been something called "the method of gaining the advantage"; but while it may be spoken of throughout the arts, swordsmanship should not be limited to this proposition alone. Swordsmanship is difficult to know simply by the advantage gained from it generally. Nor, of course, is it at all suitable to the laws of warfare.

When you look at the world, the various arts have been tailored to be items for sale. Likewise, a person thinks of himself as something to be sold and even the implements of these Ways are proffered as merchandise. This mentality divides the flower and fruit into two, and makes much less of the fruit than the flower. In this Way of the Martial Arts, especially, form is made into ornament, the flower is forced into bloom and technique is made into display: one talks of this or that dojo, teaching this Way or that Way, in an attempt to gain some benefit. Someone has said that "the immature martial art is a source of great injury," and this is certainly the truth.

Generally speaking, people make their way through the world in four Ways: the Way of the Warrior, the Farmer, the Artisan or the Merchant. Those who follow the Way of the Farmer prepare various farming implements, carefully regard the changing of the four seasons and, in this continuum, live out their days. This is the Way of the Farmer. Following the Way of the Merchant, the man who makes saké seeks out various methods of production, makes a profit from its good or poor quality and thus earns his living. In whatever way the merchant takes, he does the work appropriate to him and makes his way through the world by making a profit. This is the Way of the Merchant. As for the warrior, he prepares for himself the weapons of the various military practices and must sufficiently determine the proper uses of those weapons. This is what must be done in the Way of the Warrior. Without the preparation of weapons and an understanding of the advantages of each one, wouldn't the accomplishments of the warrior clans lose a bit of their depth? Following the Way of the Artisan, the carpenter, for example, skillfully prepares all the different kinds of tools, learns the best way of using each one, takes out his carpenter's square, works correctly according to the plans, does his work unfailingly and makes his way through the world.

These, then, are the four Ways—Warrior, Farmer, Artisan, Merchant.

I will describe the martial arts in comparison with the Way of the Carpenter. For the sake of such a comparison, let us take houses as our example. We speak of aristocratic houses; warrior houses; the four houses of the Fujiwara;[4] the destruction or continued existence of these houses or, for that matter, of a style, tradition or particular house. By using the word "house," we can make a comparison with the Way of the Carpenter. The word "carpenter" is written with the Chinese characters for "great skill." It is this "great skill" in the Way of the Martial Arts that leads me to choose the example of the carpenter.

To learn about the principles of battle, meditate on this book; for the teacher is the needle, the student the thread. As a student, you should practice without end.

COMPARING THE WAY OF THE MARTIAL ARTS TO THE CARPENTER

Like a master carpenter, the commanding general understands the measure of the empire, ascertains that of his own province and knows the gauge of his own clan. This is the Way of the master carpenter. The master carpenter clearly understands the measurement of temples, pagodas and monasteries; he knows the plans for imperial palaces and towers; he manages people and he builds houses. In this, the master carpenter and the manager of the warrior clans are the same.

In building a house, there is the problem of the selection of wood. Wood that is straight, without knots and with a good appearance, will be used for the front pillars. Wood that has a few knots but is straight and strong will be used for the rear pillars. And wood that may be a bit weak, but has no knots and is pleasing to the sight will be used variously for doorsills, lintels, doors and sliding doors. For wood that is both knotty and warped but strong, if each place needing strength in the house is discerned, it may be used after careful examination, and that house should stand for a long time. Moreover, if among the lumber there is such that is knotty, warped and weak, it will be used as scaffolding and later as kindling.

In using his carpenters, a master carpenter should know the relative quality of their skills and put them to work variously building the alcove, the doors and sliding doors, or nothing more than the doorsills, lintels and ceiling. He has the unskillful ones fix the floor joists, and those even less skilled plane the wedges. If the master carpenter understands the men well and uses them accordingly, the work will progress and the performance will be well done. The progression of the work, good performance, never-slackening attention, knowing the utility of things and the relative spirits of the men, plus giving encouragement—all such things are within the master carpenter's frame of mind. The principles of the martial arts are like this.

THE WAY OF THE MARTIAL ARTS

Liken the soldier to a carpenter. The latter sharpens his tools with his own hands, prepares the various instruments of his trade, keeps them in his carpenter's box, receives the master carpenter's instructions, shapes the pillars and beams with his adze, shaves the alcove and shelving with his plane, is accurate in spacing and carving, ascertains correct measurements and performs his duties well, down to the smallest detail. Doing this, he will later become a master carpenter himself. It is essential that the carpenter's aim be to carry equipment that will cut well and, when he has time, to sharpen that equipment. That he is an expert at taking that equipment and using it to make bookshelves, desks, and even lamps, and cutting boards and pot lids is the specialty of the carpenter. A man who is a soldier is like this. He should examine these similarities carefully. For a carpenter to achieve his aim, it is essential that his work not be uneven, that the corners fit perfectly, that the wood be well shaved with his plane, that he not polish or hone too far and that he produce work that will not twist or warp later on. If you think you would study this Way, you should be mindful of everything written here and you should examine it carefully.

THE DIVISION OF THIS BOOK INTO FIVE CHAPTERS

In order to divide this book on the Martial Arts into five Ways and show their principles chapter by chapter, I have entitled the five chapters Earth, Water, Fire, Wind and Emptiness.

In "The Earth Chapter," I provide an outline of the Way of the Martial Arts and the view of my own style. It is truly difficult to grasp the Way by swordsmanship alone. By knowing the large, you know the small; and from the shallow, you reach the deep. By drawing out a straight road over the topography, I have thus named this opening chapter, "The Earth Chapter."

The second is "The Water Chapter." Taking water as a model, one makes the mind like water. Water follows the form of either an angular or round container; it becomes either a drop or a great sea. Water is blue—its purity carrying the course of my own style in this chapter. If you discern the principles of swordsmanship with certainty, when you defeat a single opponent freely, you will have defeated everyone in the world. The mind that defeats one man is the same for innumerable opponents. The martial art of a commanding general makes the small into the large. Similarly, one may take something only a foot high and build it into a great Buddha. It is difficult to write of the significance of this in small details. With the one, know the ten thousand—this is the principle of the martial arts, and an aspect of my own style I set down in this chapter.

"The Fire Chapter" comes third. In this chapter, I note the matter of battle. I write about battle here because, like a fire, it can be large or small. So, too, can it display remarkable energy. In the Way of Battle, a confrontation between individuals and a confrontation in which ten thousand oppose ten thousand are the same. Enlarging the mind and contracting the mind—you should look at this and examine it well. It is easy to see what is large and difficult to see what is small. The reason for this is that a large group of people is difficult to change quickly, but an individual has but one mind, and that can change speedily. Thus, it is difficult to know the small. You should examine this well. Because the situation is one of an instant, this chapter deals with daily training and, as each moment is considered a decisive one, with not letting the mind go slack. These are the essentials of the martial arts. For this reason it is in this chapter that I write about victory or defeat in battle.

"The Wind Chapter," the fourth chapter, is not about my own style but rather about the other martial arts and their various styles. The Chinese character for "wind" also means "style" and, as there are ancient styles, modern styles and styles in the various schools, I will here clearly explain the martial arts in this country as well as the techniques of their various styles. This is Wind, or Style. If you do not know others, it is difficult to understand yourself. There are always heretical understandings, no matter in what Way or affair you conduct yourself. If you put your energy into such an understanding day by day, but your mind is wide of the mark, although you may think that this is a good Way, you will not be on the true path when seen from the correct position. If you do not attain the True Way, a small warp of the mind will later become a large one. You should investigate this. It is natural that others see the martial arts in swordsmanship alone. But in the principles and techniques of my martial art there is another significance. I write this chapter to inform you about other martial arts in the world, and other styles.

I write the fifth chapter, "The Emptiness Chapter," as "emptiness." With the mention of this word I am not speaking of something akin to an "interior" or an "entrance." Having attained the principles, you leave them. For in the Way of the Martial Arts there is a natural freedom: you naturally gain an extraordinary strength, you know the rhythm of the moment, you strike naturally and you hit naturally. These things are all contained in the Way of Emptiness. I write "The Emptiness Chapter" so that you might naturally enter the Way of Truth.

NAMING THE TWO-SWORD STYLE

We speak of "two swords" because warriors—both commanders and soldiers—wear two swords at their waists from the very beginning. Long ago they were called *tachi* and *katana*, but they are now called *katana* and *wakizashi*.[5] It is not necessary to write out in detail why a warrior wears these two at his waist. In our country, it is the Way of the Warrior to wear them whether the reason is understood or not. I call this the Two-Sword Style in order to express its principle. The spear, the halberd and other weapons are peripheral but are among the implements of battle. In the way of this style, it is correct for even the beginner to hold a sword and short sword in either hand and train in the Way. When you put your life on the line, you want all your weapons to be of use. Your real intent should not be to die with weapons uselessly worn at your waist. Moreover, when you hold a single weapon with both hands, it is difficult for the right and left hands to move freely. For this reason, I would have you learn to hold a sword with one hand. With a spear or halberd, there is no other way but with two hands, but the sword and short sword are both weapons to be held with one hand. It is wrong to hold a sword with both hands: it is wrong to do this on horseback and wrong to do it when you are running. This is so, whether in swamps, deep rice paddies, steep roads or in the midst of a group of people. A bow, spear or any other kind of weapon you may hold in your left hand, but in all such cases, you will have to use the sword with one hand. Thus, it is not the True Way to take a stance with a single sword with both hands. If there is a time when it is difficult to strike or kill an opponent with one hand, then you may strike him down with two.

This should not be a time-consuming event. To learn how to wield a sword in one hand, first take up two swords. This is the way to learn how to hold the sword single-handed.

A sword feels heavy and difficult to wield for anyone at first. A bow is also difficult to draw, and a halberd difficult to swing. But you get used to any weapon: for the bow, you gain strength, and if you practice with the sword you will gain strength in its Way, and come to handle it well.

The Way of the Sword is not in handling it with speed. I will cover this in "The Water Chapter." The sword is handled in open spaces, and the short sword is handled in narrow spaces. This is most fundamental to the Way. In this style, you win with either the long or the short. For this reason, the length of a sword is not predetermined. The Way of this style is the mind that obtains the victory with anything at all. It is advantageous to hold two swords rather than one, whether you are singly fighting a group of people or are confined to a narrow space. It is not necessary to write in detail about such things now. You should know the ten thousand by means of the one. When you gain the ability to act in the Way of the Martial Arts, you will miss nothing. You should investigate this thoroughly.

UNDERSTANDING THE SIGNIFICANCE OF THE WORDS "MARTIAL ARTS"[6]

In this Way, a man who is able to handle a sword is known in the world as a martial artist. Through all of the warrior's arts (芸), if one can shoot the bow well, he is called an archer; if he is skilled with a rifle, he is called a marksman; if he is able to handle a spear, he is called a spearman; and if he has learned the halberd, he is called a halberdier. However, a man who has learned the Way of the Sword is not called a practitioner of the sword or short sword. The bow, the rifle, the spear, the halberd are all weapons of the military houses and are all included in the Way of the Martial Arts (法). But there is a reason why the sword is called *the* Martial Art on its own. It is by virtue of the sword that both society and oneself are put in order, and thus it is the sword from which the martial arts originate. If a man obtains the virtue of the sword, he can singly defeat ten men. If one man can singly defeat ten men, then one hundred men can defeat one thousand, and one thousand can defeat ten thousand. In this way, in my style of the martial arts, one man or ten thousand men are the same, and each and every one of the practices of a warrior are called "martial arts."

Concerning the Way—Confucianists, Buddhists, tea masters, masters of ceremonial practices, Noh dramatists and such—none of these are within the Way of the Warrior. Even though their Ways are not ours, if you know the Way broadly, not one of them will be misunderstood. It is essential that each person polish his own Way well.

UNDERSTANDING THE VALUE OF ARMOR

In understanding the value of the implements of battle, you see that each one, according to the time or occasion, communicates its own meaning. The short sword often has advantage when you draw close to your opponent in a narrow place. The sword (long sword) can be used in any place at all and is efficient on a large scale. The halberd is thought to be inferior to the spear on the battlefield. The spear acts as an advance guard, while the halberd is used as a rear guard. Within the same degree of training, the spear is a bit stronger; but both the spear and the halberd are used according to circumstances, and have little advantage in narrow places. They are not appropriate when you are at close quarters with your opponent. They are only weapons for the battlefield, but in battle they are essential.

Nevertheless, to learn these principles indoors, to study all the minor details and to forget the Way of the actuality, will likely be of little use at all. The bow is useful on the battlefield and in the advance and retreat of troops. The bow can deal quickly with coordinated movements of spear divisions or any others, and so is an excellent weapon on an open battlefield. However, it is insufficient when attacking a castle or when the distance from the enemy exceeds twenty *ken*.[7]

These days, in all of the arts—including that of the bow—there are many flowers but little fruit. Such arts will not be found useful when the essential moment arrives and will have few advantages.[8] From inside a castle, there is nothing better than a firearm. Even on an open battlefield firearms have many advantages before the battle begins, but they are insufficient once the battle has been joined. One of the virtues of the bow is that the released arrow can be watched by the eye. The rifle bullet cannot be watched, and this is a weak point. You should investigate this matter thoroughly.

As for horses, it is essential that they have stamina and not be vicious. As with all weapons, a horse should move with a robust stride, a sword or short sword should cut cleanly, spears and halberds should thrust well, and bows and rifles should be strong and durable.

But with weapons, just as with other things, you should not make distinctions or preferences. Going too far is the same as not going far enough. Without imitating others, you should take what is appropriate to yourself and use a weapon you can handle. It is wrong for either general or soldier to have a preference for one thing and to dislike another. It is essential to make efforts in these things.

THE RHYTHM OF MARTIAL ARTS

There is a rhythm to everything, but particularly in the martial arts, if you do not train in its rhythm it is difficult to succeed. To indicate some of the rhythms in the world, there are those for the Way of Noh drama. When the rhythms of the musicians playing wind and stringed instruments are coordinated, the entire rhythm is balanced. In the military arts, there is a rhythm and timing in the release of the bow, in the firing of a rifle and even in mounting a horse. You cannot ignore rhythm in any of the arts and accomplishments.

Moreover, there is rhythm in the formless. Concerning the position of a warrior, there is a rhythm to rising in the service of his lord, and a rhythm for retreating from it; there is a rhythm to being in harmony with others, and a rhythm to not being in harmony with them. In the Way of the Merchant, there is a rhythm for becoming a wealthy man, and a rhythm for ruining oneself with wealth. The rhythm is different according to each and every Way. You should discriminate thoroughly between the rhythm of success and the rhythm of failure.

There are various rhythms to the martial arts. First, know the rhythm of balance [vis-à-vis your opponent], and be able to distinguish the rhythm of imbalance. Within the rhythms of large and small, slow and fast, know the rhythm of contact, the rhythm of spacing as well as the rhythm of resistance to rhythm. These are essential to the martial arts. If you are unable to discern the rhythm of resistance to your opponent's rhythm, your martial art will not be correct. In a battle of martial arts, victory is in knowing the rhythms of your various opponents, in using a rhythm your opponent will be unable to grasp and in developing a rhythm of emptiness (空) rather than one of wisdom.

In each of these chapters, I write most principally of this matter of rhythm. You should investigate what is written here and train yourself thoroughly.

As for the Way of the above style of martial art, by endeavoring to put it into practice morning and evening, day in and day out, your mind should broaden of itself and you will have a martial art for either large groups of men or individuals. Passing this on to the world, I now write this down for the first time in the five chapters of Earth, Water, Fire, Wind and Emptiness.

For those who would study my martial art, there are rules for putting it into practice:

1. Think without any dishonesty.
2. Forge yourself in the Way.
3. Touch upon all of the arts.
4. Know the Ways of all occupations.

5. Know the advantages and disadvantages of everything.

6. Develop a discerning eye in all matters.

7. Understand what cannot be seen by the eye.

8. Pay attention to even small things.

9. Do not involve yourself with the impractical.

Generally speaking, you should put your mind to these principles in this manner and train yourself in the Way of the Martial Arts. In this Way alone, if you do not take a broad field of vision towards what is true, it will be difficult to become an accomplished martial artist. If you are able to learn these rules, it will be a Way in which you should not be defeated, even alone against twenty or thirty opponents. If you will first and foremost keep your attention unfailingly on the martial arts and exert yourself in the correct Way, you will defeat others with a strike of the hand or overcome others by the power of perception. Again, if through your training you can freely move your entire body at will, you will defeat others with this body. And if your mind becomes trained in this Way, you will defeat others with your mind. Extending yourself this far, how could this be a Way for your own defeat?

Again, as a martial art for large numbers, this Way will excel in supplying good men as soldiers and in using numbers of those men; it will excel as a Way to carry yourself correctly; and it will excel in regulating the country, in maintaining the people and in establishing order in society. You will know how not to fall behind others in any of the other Ways, how to help your own self and how to establish your reputation. This is the Way of the Martial Arts.

Twelfth Day of the Fifth Month, Second Year of Shoho
Shinmen Musashi

THE WATER
CHAPTER

The heart of the martial art of the Two-Heavens Style takes water as its foundation and exercises the practice of advantage. Because of this, I have named this "The Water Chapter," and here write about the swordsmanship of this style.

This Way is, in all regards, difficult to write about in detail with the mind just as it is. But even if the words do not seem to connect, you should be able to perceive its principles naturally. You should deeply consider what is written in this book, word by word, character by character. If you think about it indifferently, you are likely to diverge from the Way many times. Concerning the principles of the martial arts, there may be many places where they are described in the manner of a contest of individuals, but it is essential that you understand these principles to be for a battle of opposing armies of ten thousand men, as well, and that you see them in a large way.

In this Way, especially, if you misperceive it or become lost just a little, you will fall into distortion. You will not reach the essence of the martial arts by merely looking at this book. Think that what is written down here was done just for you, and do not consider simply looking at it, familiarizing yourself with it or trying to imitate it. Rather, you should consider these principles as though they were discovered from your own mind, and continually make great efforts to make them a physical part of yourself.

THE FRAME OF MIND FOR THE MARTIAL ARTS

In the Way of the Martial Arts, do not let your frame of mind be any different from your everyday mind. In both everyday and military events, your mind should not change in the least, but should be broad and straightforward, neither drawn too tight nor allowed to slacken even a little. Keep the mind in the exact center, not allowing it to become sidetracked; let it sway peacefully, not allowing it to stop doing so for even a moment. You should investigate these things thoroughly.

Do not let your mind stand still even when you are in repose, but do not let it speed up even when you are involved in quick actions. The mind should not be distracted by the body, nor the body distracted by the mind. Be very watchful of the mind, but less so of the body; let the mind be replete without being the least bit overloaded. Though the mind appears weak on the surface, it should be strong at the bottom. Act so that your opponent cannot understand your mind. The man whose body is small should bear everything in mind about the man whose body is large, and the man whose body is large should bear everything in mind about the man whose body is small. But whether the body be large or small, keep the mind straight and in a way that it will allow no personal preferences. All these things are essential.

Do not let the mind become clouded inside; keep it broad, and place your wisdom in that broad place. It is very important to polish both wisdom and mind earnestly.

Sharpen your wisdom, distinguish principle and its opposite in the world, learn the good and bad of all things, experience all the arts and accomplishments and their various Ways, and act in a way so that you will not be taken in by anyone. This is the heart of the wisdom of the martial arts.

There is something particularly unique in the wisdom of the martial arts. Even when the action is extraordinarily lively on the battlefield, you should take the principles of the martial arts to the extreme and keep your mind unmoved. You should investigate this thoroughly.

APPEARANCE IN THE MARTIAL ARTS

In body posture, your face is neither turned down nor turned up, it is neither turned to the side nor distorted. Your eyes are not confused and your brow is not knit; narrow the space between your eyebrows, and do not move your eyeballs at all. Narrow the eyes a little without expressing a glimmer. With your face tranquil and the line of your nose straight, you should have a slight sensation of sticking your chin out. The line of the back of your neck is straight. Put strength into the nape of your neck, and think of your body as one from the shoulders down. Drop both shoulders, keep your back straight, do not stick out your rear and put strength from your knees to the front of your feet. Extend your stomach so that your hips will not be bent. To tighten the wedge, so to speak, the scabbard of your short sword should be carried at the belly and the sash tied so that it will not loosen. This is the teaching of "tightening the wedge."

In all things concerning the body in the martial arts, make the everyday body the body for the martial arts, and the body for the martial arts the everyday body. This is essential and should be examined thoroughly.

USING THE EYES IN THE MARTIAL ARTS

In using the eyes, do so in a large and encompassing way. There is observation and there is seeing.[1] The eye of observation is strong. The eye of seeing is weak. To see the faraway as nearby, and the nearby as faraway is essential to the martial arts. To know your opponent's sword, yet not to "see"[2] it at all is very important in the martial arts. You should make great efforts in this. The use of the eyes is the same for martial events whether in individual combat or in large confrontations. It is essential that your eyes do not move and that you be able to see on both sides. It is difficult to understand such a thing when, suddenly, the situation becomes chaotic. Learn what is written in this book, master the use of the eyes and do not change that use under any circumstances. This is something you should investigate thoroughly.

THE WAY TO HOLD A SWORD

To grasp a sword, give your thumb and index fingers a sense of flotation. Keep your middle finger neither tight nor loose, and tighten your ring and little fingers. It is wrong to have a relaxed grasp; you should take up the sword with the idea of cutting your opponent down. When you do this, you should hold your sword so that there is no change in your grasp nor the possibility of your hand contracting into an uncontrollable position. Whether you are bracing, parrying, striking or restraining your opponent's sword, you should be intent on moving only your thumb and index finger a little. In all events, grasp your sword with the intent of cutting the man down. Your grasp does not change when doing this, whether the act involves the testing of new swords on prisoners or corpses, or is taking place in a real fight. In all things, whether it be the sword or the hand, immobility is undesirable. Immobility means a dead hand; mobility means a living hand. You should understand this well.

USE OF THE FEET

In the carriage of the feet, you should float your toenails a little and step strongly with your heels. In the use of the feet, you should walk as usual, whether the case calls for large, small, quick or slow strides. Feet that seem to fly, float or be immobile are, all three, undesirable.

There is something important in this Way called the Yin-Yang Foot, and it is considered essential. The Yin-Yang Foot means never moving just one foot. With Yin-Yang, you step right and left, right and left, whether striking, pulling back or parrying a blow. I repeat: you should never step with just one foot. You should investigate this thoroughly.

THE FIVE STANCES

The Five Stances include the Upper, the Middle, the Lower, the Right-Side Stance and the Left-Side Stance. The stances are divided into five, but they are all for the purpose of cutting a man down. There are no other than these five. No matter which of these stances you take, you should not think of the stance itself, but rather that you are going to cut your opponent down.

Whether a stance is large or small, it should follow the circumstances and the advantage you wish to take. The Middle, Upper and Lower are stances of the body; the two side stances

A self-portrait attributed to Musashi

are stances of free and easy motion. The Left-Side and Right-Side Stances are those used to check the area above you and to the two sides. For their use, you should judge according to the circumstances. You should understand that in this Way, it is largely said that the Middle Stance is the best. The main intention of the stance itself is found in the Middle Stance. Look at the martial arts in terms of large armies. The Middle Stance is the seat of the commanding general, and the four other Stances follow after him. You should investigate this thoroughly.

THE WAY OF THE SWORD

"Knowing the Way of the Sword" means that, even when you handle with two fingers what I generally indicate as the sword,[3] you understand what you are doing and can handle it freely. You go against the Way of the Sword by trying to handle it with speed, and it will be difficult to wield. To the extent that you handle the sword well, you will handle it tranquilly. If you think you will handle it with speed, as you would a fan or a dagger, you will not be in accord with the Way of the Sword, and it will be difficult to wield. Using what is called a knife cut, you will be unable to cut a man down with a sword.

If you have struck downward with your sword, raise it in a simple way; if you have swung it to the side, return it to the other side in a simple way. But in all cases, extend your elbow fully, and swing with strength. This is the Way of the Sword.

If you learn to use the Five Fundamentals, or Stances, of my martial art, the Way of the Sword will be in order and you will handle it well. You should practice this thoroughly.

CONCERNING THE FIRST OF THE FIVE FUNDAMENTALS

The Middle Stance, where the tip of the sword is aimed at your opponent's face, is the first of the Five Fundamentals. When you meet with your opponent and he strikes with his sword, deflect it to the right. When he strikes at you again, strike so that the tip of his sword returns upward and leave your sword, which has swung downward, in just that position. When your opponent attacks again, strike his hands from below. This is the first.

All of these Five Fundamentals are difficult to understand just by what is written here. For the Five Fundamentals, you train in the Way of the Sword with your hands. With these five techniques of using the sword, you will know my Way of the Sword and will be able to understand your opponent's sword, no matter how he strikes. This is why I am teaching you that, with two swords, there are no other than these Five Stances. You should put them into practice.

CONCERNING THE SECOND FUNDAMENTAL

In the second use of the sword, take the Upper Stance and strike your opponent at the same moment he makes his attack to strike you. If you have struck at your opponent but missed him, leave your sword just as it is, and when he strikes again, strike him by bringing your sword back up. This will be the same for yet another strike.

There are various frames of mind and rhythms to take within these fundamental stances. Practice this style within their framework, and you will know the five Ways of the Sword in detail. Thus, you will win in any situation. You should put them into practice.

CONCERNING THE THIRD FUNDAMENTAL

In the Third Fundamental, use the Lower Stance, with an idea of drawing your opponent in. When he advances to strike, you strike his hands from below. At the point when you are to strike his hand, your opponent may once again advance to strike. As he goes to knock down your sword, let his excessive rhythm pass, then cut his upper arm laterally after he has made his strike. With the Lower Stance, you kill the opponent at the same moment he strikes.

For training in the Way, the Lower Stance is fitting for both the beginner and the more experienced alike. You should take up the sword and practice.

CONCERNING THE FOURTH FUNDAMENTAL

In the Fourth Stance, you should take a position with the sword held laterally to the left, striking your opponent's sword hand from below. As your opponent moves to strike down on your upward strike, stay intent on striking his hand, parry the path of his sword immediately, then cut obliquely in the direction of·

your shoulder. This is the Way of the Sword. Again, it is a means of winning by parrying the path of your opponent's sword as he strikes. You should investigate this thoroughly.

CONCERNING THE FIFTH FUNDAMENTAL

In the Fifth Fundamental, you should take a stance with your sword held laterally to your right. As your opponent comes to strike, change the path of your sword from the lower side, raise it to the upper position and immediately cut down from above. This is also for the purpose of knowing the Way of the Sword well. If you get used to wielding the sword with this fundamental stance, you will be able to handle a heavy sword easily.

I have not written in detail about these Five Fundamentals. To know my style in general, to gain a larger understanding of its rhythm and to be able to discern the direction of your opponent's sword, it is essential to first polish these Five Fundamentals daily.

By earnestly applying these paths of the sword, by seeing through your opponent's intent and by using these various rhythms, even as you fight with your opponent, you will win in one way or another. You should understand this thoroughly.

THE LESSON OF THE STANCE-NO-STANCE

The so-called Stance-No-Stance calls for no stance at all to be taken with your sword. However, as I place this within the Five Stances, there is a stance here. According to the chances your opponent takes, and his position and energy, your sword will be of a mind to cut him down in fine fashion no matter where you place it. According to the moment, if you want to lower your sword a little from the Upper Stance, it will become a Middle Stance; if, according to the situation, you raise your sword a bit from the Middle Stance, it will become the Upper Stance. Likewise, the Lower Stance may be raised a little to become the Middle Stance. This means that the two Side Stances, depending on their position, may be moved a little to the center to become either the Middle or Lower Stance.

This is the principle in which there is, and there is not, a stance. At its heart, this is first taking up the sword and then cutting down your opponent, no matter what is done or how it happens. Whether you parry, slap, strike, hold back or touch your opponent's cutting sword, you must understand that all of these are opportunities to cut him down. To think, "I'll parry" or "I'll slap" or "I'll hit, hold or touch" will be insufficient for cutting him down. It is essential to think that anything at all is an opportunity to cut him down. You should investigate this thoroughly. With martial arts in the larger field, the placement of numbers of people is also a stance. All of these are opportunities to win a battle. It is wrong to be inflexible. You should make great efforts in this.

STRIKING YOUR OPPONENT IN ONE COUNT

The Rhythm of Striking an Opponent in One Count means taking a position within which both you and your opponent may strike each other and, before he has settled on a tactic and without moving your body or putting your mind anywhere, striking him quickly and directly. Striking with this rhythm before your opponent has even considered pulling back his sword, avoiding a blow or striking with his sword is the "one count." You should learn this well, practicing to strike quickly in the rhythm of the interval.

THE DOUBLE-ACTION RHYTHM

In the Double-Action Rhythm,[4] when you advance to strike your opponent and he quickly moves back and then strikes, feign your next move by first striking at the point where he has completed his action, then strike once again at the point of his withdrawal. This is the Double-Action Rhythm.

It will be rather difficult to master this stroke by merely following what is written here. But once having received this lesson, you will quickly come to understand it.

THE NO THOUGHT–NO CONCEPT STRIKE

When you think that both you and your opponent are ready to strike, your body becomes a striking body, your mind becomes a striking mind and your hand instantaneously strikes with strength emerging from nothingness and leaving no wake. This is the most important strike, that of No Thought–No Concept. This is often an effective strike, and you should practice and master it thoroughly.

THE STRIKE OF RUNNING WATER

Should you and your opponent be equally matched, and should he attempt to quickly move away, avoid your strike and brush your sword away, you must inflate both body and mind, let your sword follow your body and, quite slowly, strike with all the power of momentarily restrained water bursting forth from a running stream. This I call the Strike of Running Water. When you master this, you will have, with certainty, a good strike. It is essential to discern your opponent's position.

THE CONNECTION HIT

When you are about to strike your opponent and he tries to either parry or brush the stroke aside, hit his head, hand and foot in one stroke. The Connection Strike describes a strike made any place at all with one path of your sword. Learn this strike well; it will be effective at any time. Use this in fights often, and you will understand it.

THE FLINT-AND-SPARK HIT

The Flint-and-Spark Hit is executed by striking with great certainty and strength, without raising your sword at all, when your sword is joined with your opponent's. You should put strength into your feet, body and hands, and strike quickly with these three.

THE AUTUMN-LEAF STRIKE

The heart of the Autumn-Leaf Strike is in striking down your opponent's sword and picking it up yourself. When your opponent takes a stance in front of you and is intent on striking, hitting or parrying with his sword, strike his sword strongly with either the No Thought–No Concept Strike or the Flint-and-Spark Strike in mind. In the same moment, without letting up for a second, if you hit him again with the lowered point of your weapon, he will invariably drop his sword.

THE BODY TAKING THE PLACE OF THE SWORD

This could also be called the Sword Taking the Place of the Body. As a rule, when you strike at your opponent, you do not strike with both body and sword at the same time. Depending on the circumstances of your opponent's attack, you use your body first in the strike, causing your sword to then strike regardless of your body. Though it may be that, without moving your body, you strike with your sword, for the most part, the body strikes first and is followed by the strike of the sword. You should investigate this thoroughly and put it into practice.

THE STRIKE AND THE HIT

The Strike and the Hit are two different things. The heart of what is called a Strike—no matter what kind of Strike—is to do so consciously and with certainty. A Hit is when you have advanced toward and collided with your opponent, even when, by virtue of your strength, he dies immediately. This is a Hit. A Strike is executed consciously. You should examine this. Whether you are going for your opponent's hand or foot, the Hit comes first. This is so that after the Hit you can strike with strength. Hitting may be understood as touching. When you have learned this well, it is a special thing. You should make efforts in this.

THE BODY OF THE *SHUKO*

The essence of this technique is that the *shuko* does not extend his arms.[5] When you advance toward your opponent, do not have the least thought of extending your arms, but rather rush in quickly before he strikes. If you think of extending your arms, your body will retract. Thus, be intent on entering quickly and striking with your entire body. It is easy to approach with your body in the same time it would take for your hand to reach out. You should investigate this thoroughly.

THE BODY OF LACQUER AND GLUE

The essence of Lacquer and Glue is that when you have come close to the body of your opponent, stick to it without separating. When you have closed in on your opponent's body, stick to it with strength—head, body and feet. Often people will close in with their head or feet but will leave out the rest of their body. Keep your body pressed to your opponent's, without letting even a small space in between. You should investigate this thoroughly.

COMPARING STATURE

Comparing Stature refers to the avoidance of contracting your body in any way whenever you have closed in on an opponent. Close in with strength—extending your legs, waist and neck—and align your face with that of your opponent. In measuring yourself up to him, be intent on exceeding him. You will then gain in height and rush in with strength. You should make great efforts with this.

APPLYING GLUE

When you and your opponent strike together and he has checked your blow, continue to apply your sword to his as if you were applying glue, and close in. The essence of this stickiness is to make it difficult for your swords to separate, but you must be mindful not to use too much strength. When you make contact with your opponent's sword, apply the glue and close in; do so with great tranquillity and you will feel no distress. The difference between being sticky and being entangled is that stickiness is strong and entanglement is weak. You should make a distinction between the two.

THE BODY BLOW

The Body Blow is executed by closing in on your opponent and hitting him with your body the split second before he takes action. Turn your face a little to the side, extend your left shoulder and hit your opponent's chest. The action of hitting him should be done with great bodily force, with breathing and rhythm and while being mindful to close in with momentum. When you grasp this way of closing, you will become strong enough to throw a person back a great distance.

You will be able to hit him with such strength that he dies. You should practice this well.

THREE PARRIES

When closing in on your opponent and parrying the sword with which he strikes, make as if to stab him in the eye with your own sword. Then, draw his sword toward your right shoulder. This is the first parry. The next, the "stabbing parry," involves parrying the sword your opponent strikes with by making as if to stab his right eye, then stabbing him with the intention of jamming your sword into his neck. Again, when your opponent strikes, close in on him with a short sword[6] and, without much regard for the sword that you parry, close in as if to strike your opponent's face with your left hand.

These are the Three Parries. Keep in mind the tightening of your left hand and making as if to strike your opponent's face with your fist. This is something you should practice thoroughly.

STABBING THE FACE

When you have faced off with your opponent and your swords are equally set, it is essential that you be constantly intent on stabbing his face with the tip of your sword. If you keep your mind on stabbing your opponent's face, he will pull his face and body back. If you can make him do this, you will have various advantages for victory. You should make thorough efforts in this.

In the midst of the fight, if you are intent on making your opponent flinch, you will have already obtained the victory. For this reason, you should not forget about stabbing at your opponent's face. Among the disciplines of the martial arts, this is a principle you should practice.

STABBING THE HEART

Stabbing the Heart means that in the midst of a fight, when you are obstructed both above and at the side and are completely unable to slash your opponent, you should stab him. The instant you are aware of having evaded his striking sword, expose the ridge[7] of your sword directly at your opponent, draw back so that the tip does not waver and stab him in the chest. If you have become tired, or your sword will not cut, this technique can be used exclusively. You should understand this thoroughly.

KATSU-TOTSU

For *Katsu-Totsu*,[8] when making your attack and closing in on your opponent—and he, in turn, goes to make a counterattack—raise your sword as if to stab him from below and strike him in return. Both actions should be done with a quick rhythm, striking with a *Katsu-Totsu*: that is, *Katsu* when you make your rising stab, *Totsu* when you strike. Whenever you are in the middle of an exchange of blows, this rhythm is particularly fitting.

The proper execution of *Katsu-Totsu* is to keep a sense of stabbing your opponent as you raise the tip of your sword, but then, in that very instant, to strike him. That is the rhythm. You should practice and investigate this well.

SLAP AND PARRY

The Slap and Parry is used when you are engaged with an opponent and the rhythm becomes one of just banging away at cross-purposes. When your opponent strikes, you slap and meet his sword with yours. The heart of slapping and meeting is not simply in a fierce slap or a simple parry. In responding to your opponent's sword, you slap it as it strikes and then, immediately, you strike your opponent. The essence of this is that you take the offensive with both the slap and the strike.

If your slap is done with a good rhythm, even with small intent, the tip of your sword will not fall no matter how hard your opponent strikes.

ENCOUNTERING MANY OPPONENTS

Encountering Many Opponents is of concern when you alone are engaged against a large number of men. Unsheathe both sword and short sword, open left and right arms broadly, and take a stance with your swords tilted laterally.

Even when your opponents come at you from all directions, be of a mind to drive them into one place. When your opponents attack, see clearly who is in front of you and who behind. Quickly engage the man or men advancing in front of you, but watch peripherally and understand the position of your opponents. Handle the sword in your right hand and the sword in your left at one time, but independently. It is not good to hesitate. The essence of this is to quickly take stances toward your opponents on both sides; where opponents come forth, cut into them vigorously and put them into disorder; then immediately charge to where other opponents advance and rout them as well. Above all, be intent on driving your opponents into one direction like a school of fish. When you see that they are falling all over each other, you should wade into them vigorously and without any pause.

If you do not chase in directly toward the place where your opponents have gathered, you will not make progress. And, if you start thinking about the direction from which your opponents will come, your mind will be waiting and you will have the same result. Parry your opponents' rhythm, know where they will crumble, and you will have the victory.

From time to time practice herding your opponents into a group and chasing after them. If you understand the heart of that, you will be at ease whether your opponents number one, ten or even twenty. Investigate this and practice it well.

THE PRINCIPLE OF EXCHANGING BLOWS

The Principle of Exchanging Blows refers to being able to understand victory in terms of the martial arts and the sword. It is not in writing it down in detail. Practicing well, you will know victory. By and large, it is the sword that manifests the Way of the Martial Arts. This is an oral tradition.

ONE STRIKE

If you keep the One Strike in mind, you will assuredly gain the victory. If you do not study the martial arts well, they will be difficult to understand. If you do train yourself thoroughly in this, the Way will be there for the martial arts to develop in accordance with your mind, and for your mind to take the victory on its own. You should practice thoroughly.

DIRECT TRANSMISSION

The heart of Direct Transmission is handed down by receiving the true Way of the Two-Sword Style. It is essential that you train thoroughly and make it a part of you. This is an oral tradition.

I have recorded in this chapter the main points of the swordsmanship of the Two-Sword Style. In the martial arts, you take up the sword and learn how to overcome others.

First, with the Five Fundamentals, you gain knowledge of the Five Stances, you learn the Way of the Sword, your entire body becomes flexible, your mind becomes quick, you become skillful on your own with the sword, your body and feet work harmoniously with your mind and you move as you please. Overcoming one person or two goes according to your knowledge of right and wrong in the martial arts.

Practice what is in this book line by line, engage your opponents and gradually you will grasp the principle of the Way. Keep this unceasingly in mind, but do not be hurried; try your hand from time to time, and learn the heart of each step. And no matter whom you fight, know his mind.

The journey of a thousand *ri* proceeds step by step, so think without rushing.[9] Understanding that this is the duty of a warrior, put these practices into action, surpass today what you were yesterday, go beyond those of poor skill tomorrow and exceed those who are skillful later. You should do as is written in this book and not think in a way that will let your mind become sidetracked.

Therefore, no matter what kind of opponent you fight and defeat, by turning your back on this teaching you will not be on the True Way.

If these principles are recalled to mind, you should be able to discern how to beat any number of opponents on your own. This being so, grasp the Way of the Martial Arts with the strength of your knowledge of swordsmanship, for many opponents or only one. See to it that you temper yourself with one thousand days of practice, and refine yourself with ten thousand days of training.

You should investigate this thoroughly.

Twelfth Day of the Fifth Month, Second Year of Shoho
Shinmen Musashi

THE FIRE
CHAPTER

In the martial arts of the Two-Sword Style, I compare battle to fire. Thus I have written about the matter of contest in battle as "The Fire Chapter."

First of all, everyone in this world fancies the insignificant principles of the martial arts, whether in knowing how to give the wrist a three- to five-inch advantage with the fingertips, or in understanding how to gain the victory by extending the forearm by handling a fan. Or again, by taking up a bamboo sword or something like it, all may study the simple advantage of speed and, in learning the functions of the hands and feet, specialize in the lesser advantages of alacrity.

In my martial art, you put your life on the line many times by engaging in battle, you distinguish the principles of life and death, you study the Way of the Sword, you know the strengths and weaknesses of your opponent's striking sword, you discern the Way of the edge and back of the sword blade, and you practice how to strike and defeat your opponent. In doing this, you do not bother your thoughts with insignificant or small matters.

Above all, when it comes to the principles of bracing yourself with the six kinds of armor, you will not be thinking of insignificant techniques. Moreover, my Way of the Martial Arts is to know the Way of victory with certainty when you are fighting for your life alone against five or ten men. Accordingly, what kind of difference can there be in the principles for one man defeating ten and in those for one thousand men defeating ten thousand? You should investigate this thoroughly.

Nevertheless, gathering one thousand or ten thousand men and studying this Way is not something that can be done during ordinary times of practice. But if you only take up your sword on your own, by gauging each opponent's strategy and getting to know his strengths and weaknesses, and by virtue of your knowledge of the Martial Arts, you will plumb the depths of defeating ten thousand men and become an expert in this Way.

Who in this world can obtain my correct Way of the Martial Arts? Whoever would get to the heart of it, let him do so with conviction, practicing in the morning and training in the evening.

After he has polished his techniques and gained independent freedom of movement, he will naturally gain miraculous powers, and his free and easy strength will be wonderful. This is the spirit wherein, as a warrior, he will put these practices into action.

CONCERNING PLACE

In distinguishing the conditions of the place (of combat), the sun should be at your back. You should take up your stance with the sun behind you. If, according to the place, there is a time when you are unable to put the sun at your back, you should try to put it to your right side. It is the same even if you are in a room: the light should be behind you or to your right. You want to take your stance with no obstruction behind you, with your left side at ease, and so that you have closed off the right. To have your opponent visible even at night, you should take up your stance with the same understanding: fire should be at your rear, light should be off to your right. For looking down on your opponent, you should consider taking your stance in a slightly elevated place. In a room, you should think of the seat of honor as the elevated place.

As for chasing your opponent about in battle, it is essential that you chase him to your left, that you get the difficult terrain to his rear and that you then drive him, above all, toward those difficult places. In regard to such difficult places, do not let your opponent assess the situation; keep his face from being able to turn by attacking and checking him, leaving no moment unguarded. Even in a room, you should likewise drive your opponent toward the threshold, the lintel, the door, the *shoji*, the veranda or pillars without letting him evaluate the place.

In any case, when you drive your opponent before you, do so toward a place where there is difficult footing or some sort of obstruction at his side. It is important that you be intent to use the advantages of the place, and so gain the victory with the place itself. You should investigate this thoroughly and put it into practice.

TAKING THE THREE INITIATIVES

* The Initiative of Attack is when I attack my opponent.
* The Initiative of Waiting is when my opponent attacks me.
* The Body-Body Initiative is when both my opponent and I attack at the same time.

These are the Three Initiatives. In the beginning of any confrontation, there are no other initiatives than these three. You can quickly gain the victory according to the circumstances of these initiatives, and so they rank first in the martial arts. There are various distinctions involved with these initiatives, but you select your own according to the moment. And, as you will be victorious by seeing into your opponent's mind and by the wisdom of the martial arts, I will not write down all the details.

First, in the Initiative of Attack, when you consider attacking, remain calm, then suddenly attack first and quickly. This is an initiative in which you move your body with speed and strength, but leave plenty of margin in your mind. Moreover, while your mind is using great strength, your feet will move a little more quickly than usual. Thus, the initiative is quick and vigorous as you approach your opponent. Again, unfetter your mind and, from beginning to end, be intent on one thing: smashing your opponent. By this, your mind will be strong to its very core, and you will gain the victory. This is, in all events, the Initiative of Attack.

Second, in the Initiative of Waiting, when your opponent attacks you, stay completely unruffled, but show a weak appearance and, as he comes close, move away briskly. Looking as though you are now ready to leap away, watch for the moment he relaxes, then take the victory directly and vigorously. This is one initiative. Another is when your opponent attacks and you come on even more strongly. Here, gain the victory immediately by taking advantage of the moment his rhythm changes. These are the principles of the Initiative of Waiting.

In the Body-Body Initiative, as your opponent attacks quickly, you advance calmly but with strength; and as he approaches, your entire being quickly becomes resolved. When you see him waver, take the victory directly and with strength. Again, when your opponent attacks calmly, you attack a little more quickly, but with light and almost floating movements. When he approaches, complicate the movement a little, follow his expression and vigorously take the victory. This is the Body-Body Initiative.

This subject is difficult to write about in detail, but you should make great efforts in what I have written down here.

These Three Initiatives are used according to the moment in time and the principles involved. And, although they are not always concerned with your making the initial attack, you want to attack first and drive your opponent before you if possible. In any case, using the wisdom of the martial arts, taking the initiative is surely at the heart of gaining the victory. You should practice this thoroughly.

PRESSING DOWN THE PILLOW

Pressing Down the Pillow means not letting your opponent's head up. In the Way of Martial Arts combat, it is wrong to let your opponent lead you around or push you into a defensive position. Above all, you want to move him around freely. Therefore, as both you and your opponent are going to be mindful of this, it will be difficult for you to do if you do not perceive what he is going to do.

In the martial arts, you do such things as check your opponent's strike, suppress his stabs and break away from grappling. In what is called Pressing Down the Pillow, you grasp my True Way and, when in a confrontation, see through the indications of what your opponent is going to do regardless of his actions. When he is going to strike, before the word "strike" could even be pronounced, be intent on suppressing him and prohibit the rest of his action.

This is the heart of Pressing Down the Pillow. In "attack," for example, suppress your opponent at the letter *a*; for "leap," suppress him at the letter *l*; for "cut," suppress him at the letter *c*. This is all done with the same understanding.

In the martial arts, when your opponent is going to use some technique on you, it is important that you let him do it if it's a useless one. But, if his action is functional, suppress it and keep him from completing it.

The mind that thinks, "suppress this, suppress that," about an opponent's actions is also a mind on the defensive. First, no matter what you are involved in, entrust yourself to the Way and, while the execution of a technique is still in play, suppress what your opponent might think of doing even before the first letter of the word could be pronounced. Sustain your action over your opponent so that anything he does comes to nothing. Thus you will be an expert and forged in the martial arts. You should investigate Pressing Down the Pillow thoroughly.

FERRYING ACROSS

Ferrying Across is like crossing the sea. When you traverse a strait or make a long crossing of the sea, for a distance of even forty or fifty *ri*, you use "ferrying." In passing through this human world, too, there are likely many places within the space of a generation that may be called Ferrying Across. On a ship's course, you know where these places are, you know the capacity of the ship and you know the weather patterns well. Though other ships may not venture out, you do so by responding to the conditions of the hour, relying on either a crosswind or a tail wind and, if the wind changes, putting in the oars for two or three *ri*. With your mind set on arriving at port, you board the ship and ferry across.

You should think in terms of Ferrying Across when you pass through society and set your mind on some serious affair.

For the martial arts, Ferrying Across is essential even in the midst of battle. Here you take into account the level of your opponent, judge your own degree of expertise and, using the principles of the martial arts, ferry across. It is the same for a good mariner ferrying across a sea route.

After Ferrying Across, you again feel at ease. In Ferrying Across, you will generally gain a quick victory by bringing out the weaknesses in your opponent and taking the initiative yourself.

The intent to ferry across is essential in the martial arts whether your opponents are one or many. You should investigate this thoroughly.

KNOWING CONDITIONS

In the main current of the martial arts, Knowing Conditions means knowing where your opponents flourish or fall, knowing the number of their allies, taking in the lay of the land, clearly observing your opponents' conditions and—according to the maneuvering of your own allies and these principles of the martial arts—grasping the way of victory with certainty, understanding the degree of initiative to be taken and going into battle.

Even in solitary combat, it is essential that you discern your opponent's style, see through the character of his allies, detect his strengths and weaknesses, understand how to take him by surprise, know well the scale of his rhythm along with the rhythm of his space and time intervals, and take the initiative. Knowing Conditions is being absolutely able to make assessments when your own intellect is strong.

As you gain freedom in the martial arts, you should be able to fathom your opponent's mind well, and thus have many ways of victory. You should make efforts in this.

STEPPING ON THE SWORD

First, in martial arts on a grand scale, when our opponents fire bows and guns at our troops and then commence battle in whatever way, they first fire their weapons and then charge. If we *then* notch arrows to our bows and put powder into our firearms, it will be difficult to push through to their camp. The heart of Stepping on the Sword, something used principally in the martial arts, is that even with bows and firearms, you must act quickly *while* they are being discharged: if you charge quickly, it will be difficult to notch another arrow to a bow or discharge a firearm. In all things, when your opponent sets up a tactic, respond to it immediately according to its own principles and, stepping on his actions, defeat him.

Again, in the martial arts of one-on-one combat, if you strike only after your opponent has struck with his sword, the fight will become that of one beat after another, and you will make no progress. The idea of stepping on your opponent's striking sword with your foot is to defeat him the moment he strikes, preventing him from striking a second time.

Stepping should not be limited to your feet, but whether doing so with your body, mind or, of course, your sword, you should be intent on not giving your opponent a second chance. This is, therefore, the mind of taking the initiative in everything. It does not mean attacking at the same time as your opponent. Stepping on the Sword is taking your action immediately upon your opponent's action. You should investigate this thoroughly.

KNOWING COLLAPSE

Collapse is common to all things. The collapse of a house, the collapse of a body, the collapse of your opponent—all of them, according to the moment, are collapses from a discordance of rhythm.

In martial arts involving large numbers, it is essential to grasp the rhythm of your opponents' collapse and to hasten your offensive so that they cannot escape that moment. Escaping that moment of collapse, they will likely recover.

Again, in the martial arts of one-on-one as well, you grasp the moment of collapse in your opponent's changing rhythm during the fight. If you are negligent enough to miss this, he will recover and begin anew, and you will make no progress.

It is essential that you grasp the sign of your opponent's collapse and rush him with certainty so that he will be unable to recover. Your rushing attack must be instantaneous and strong, and you must cut him down with such vigor that he cannot recover. You should understand this "cutting down with vigor" thoroughly. If you miss this action, your mind is shilly-shallying. You should put effort into this.

BECOMING YOUR OPPONENT

Becoming Your Opponent means thinking as though your body has become that of your opponent. When you look at the world, people are apt to think that someone who has committed a robbery and has holed himself up in a house must be a strong opponent. But if you consider it from the opponent's view, he is thinking that the whole world is against him and that there is no way of escape. The man who has holed himself up in a house is a pheasant. The man who is going in to cut him down is a hawk. You should make thorough efforts in this.

Even in martial arts confrontations involving large numbers, you will be failing in something important if you think of your opponents as strong. If you have a good number of men, understand the principles of the martial arts well and believe deeply that you are going to defeat your opponents, there should be nothing to worry about.

In the martial arts of one-on-one as well, you should think in terms of Becoming Your Opponent. If he thinks you have understood the martial arts well, that you are strong in technique and that you are an expert in the Way, he is surely thinking that he is going to lose. You should investigate this thoroughly.

LETTING GO OF FOUR HANDS

Letting Go of Four Hands comes into play when both you and your opponent are of the same mind, you feel as though the fight has come to a stalemate, and you are making no progress. Thinking you have come to a stalemate, you should know enough to discard the situation immediately and gain the victory by some other method. Even in martial arts situations involving large numbers, if you are only intent on grappling, you will make no progress and will inflict injury on your allies. It is important to quickly disregard whatever you are thinking and gain the victory by some method unthought of by your opponent.

Again, even in the martial arts of one-on-one, when you think you've come to a situation of Four Hands, it is essential to change your thinking immediately, assess your opponent and understand how to gain the victory by another method. You should understand this thoroughly.

MOVING THE SHADOW

Moving the Shadow is used when you cannot see through your opponent's mind. Even in martial arts situations involving large numbers, when you cannot see through your opponents' situation in any way, act as though you were going to attack vigorously, and you will see their intentions. Once you have seen their intentions, it is an easy thing to take the victory by another method.

Again, in martial arts situations of one-on-one, when your opponent has taken a stance with his sword behind him or to his side, if you make a sudden movement as if to strike him, his thoughts will be manifested with his sword. Knowing these manifestations, you will immediately perceive a method and should know victory with certainty. If you are negligent, you will miss the rhythm. You should investigate this thoroughly.

CONTROLLING THE LIGHT

Controlling the Light[1] is applicable when you can see through your opponent's mind as he makes his attack. In martial arts situations involving large numbers, you control your opponents' tactics as they are about to execute them. If you show them that you will control their methods with strength, they will be controlled by that strength and change their minds. You can also change your mind, take the initiative from the mind of Emptiness and take the victory.[2]

Even in a martial arts situation of one-on-one, you check your opponent's strong intentions by the rhythm of your own tactic: grasp a method of victory in his checked rhythm and take the initiative.

DRAWING YOUR OPPONENT IN

Being drawn in is something common to all things. Becoming sleepy is infectious, just as yawns and such are infectious. Time, too, is infectious. In martial arts situations involving large numbers, when your opponents show themselves to be skittish and hurried, you should give an appearance of being not at all affected by this, and rather move all the more leisurely. Your opponents will then be caught up by your actions and will show signs of slackening. When you think they have been drawn in by this, attack quickly and vigorously from the mind of Emptiness and you will gain the victory.

Even in martial arts situations of one-on-one, if you act slowly with body and mind, and then catch the moment when your opponent slackens, you can take the initiative vigorously and quickly, and defeat him. This is an important point.

"Making them drunk" is something that resembles this. So

are the mentalities of boredom, skittishness and weakening. You should make great efforts in this.

AGITATING YOUR OPPONENT

There are many kinds of agitation. One is a feeling of danger, a second is a feeling that something is beyond your capability and a third is a feeling of the unexpected. You should investigate this thoroughly.

In martial arts situations involving large numbers, it is essential to agitate your opponents. It is essential that you attack violently when your opponents are not expecting it. Take advantage of the situation while their minds are unsettled, grasp the initiative and gain the victory.

Again, even in the martial arts of one-on-one, show leisureliness in the beginning, then suddenly attack vigorously. Following through on your opponent's agitation, you can take the advantage without missing a beat and grasp the victory. This is essential. You should investigate this thoroughly.

IMPOSING FEAR

Fear resides in all things, and the heart of fear is in the unexpected. In martial arts situations involving large numbers, you do not frighten your opponents with what is right before their eyes. People may be frightened by the voices of things, or they may be frightened by making the small seem large. Something frightening coming suddenly from the side also induces fear. You should grasp the rhythm of fear and gain victory by using its advantages.

Even in the martial arts of one-on-one, you can frighten an opponent with your body, you can frighten him with your sword and you can frighten him with your voice. It is essential to do this suddenly, when your opponent is not expecting it. Take advantage of his fear and gain the victory immediately. You should investigate this thoroughly.

ENTANGLING

Entangling is when you and your opponent have approached each other and clashed vigorously, and you can see that the fight is going nowhere. It is essential that at that point you immediately intertwine yourself with your opponent and, while being mixed up with him, take advantage of the situation and gain the victory.

Whether in martial arts situations involving large numbers or one-on-one, when you and your opponent are set off and then clash with mutual intent but no victory is at hand, it is important to mix in with your opponent immediately, making sure that you cannot become disentwined. Then, seize the advantage of that situation, understand how you can win on the spot and take the victory vigorously. You should investigate this thoroughly.

TOUCHING THE CORNER

Touching the Corner refers to the difficulty of forcing your way directly when pressing against anything strong. In martial arts situations involving large numbers, assess the number of your opponents, hit the corner of the place where they have struck out vigorously and you should be able to grasp the advantage. As that corner begins to lose strength, so will the entire body. It is essential that, as that strength fails, you grasp the victory by staying intent on that corner.

Even in the martial arts of one-on-one, inflict a wound on a corner of your opponent's body and, as his body grows a little weaker and begins to slump, victory will be an easy matter. You should investigate this matter thoroughly. It is important in discerning the victory.

CAUSING CONFUSION

Causing Confusion means acting so that your opponent's mind becomes uncertain. In martial arts situations involving large numbers on the battlefield, gauge your opponent's mind and, with the strength of your own wisdom in the martial arts, send his mind in different directions, make him think various things, and have him wonder if you will be slow or quick. When you grasp the rhythm of his confusion, discern your point of victory with certainty.

Again, in the martial arts of one-on-one, seize the moment and execute various techniques, feigning strikes and stabs and rushing in. When you see the signs of your opponent's confusion, take the victory freely. This is a specialty of battle. You should investigate this thoroughly.

THE THREE VOICES

The Three Voices are divided and called the Beginning, Middle and Latter Voices. Shouting is essential according to the situation. Voice adds the element of energy, so people shout at fires, great winds and large waves. Voice manifests vigor.

In martial arts situations involving large numbers, the shouts at the beginning of the battle are given as vigorously as possible to intimidate your opponents; the shouts in the middle of the battle lower the pitch and are given from the very depths; and, after defeating your opponents, another great shout is given vigorously. These are the Three Voices.

Again, even in the martial arts of one-on-one, you feign a strike and yell "*Ei!*" at the very beginning in order to incite your opponent to move. You then strike with your sword after you have yelled. Again, the yell you give after you have struck your opponent is an expression of victory. These are called the Beginning and Latter Voices.

You do not give a great yell at the same time you strike with your sword. If you yell during a battle, it is done with a low voice in order to ride its rhythm. You should investigate this thoroughly.

MIXING IN

Mixing In occurs in battles with large numbers, when the troops have clashed and you see that your opponent is strong. You Mix In when you attack one point of your opponents and, seeing that it has collapsed, you leave it and strike at other strong points. Generally, the heart of this is in zigzagging attacks.

In the martial arts on a smaller scale, this mentality is essential for when you are facing a group alone. Do not simply defeat one single opponent, but rout one after another, always attacking another strong opponent. Grasp one man's rhythm and, with your own good rhythm, zigzag to the left and right, attacking as you read your opponent's expression. When you grasp your opponent's condition and rush in, be intent on taking the victory vigorously without the least bit of a retreat.

This mentality is also for when you clash with a single strong opponent. The heart of Mixing In is in not knowing a single step of retreat and in getting lost in the crowd.

CRUSHING

Smashing your opponent completely, even if he seems weak and you are strong, is called Crushing. This mentality is important. In martial arts situations involving large numbers, when you perceive that your opponents are few in number—or even, should they be numerous—once you have confused them and found their weaknesses, you crush them. In other words, from the very beginning, you are intent on intimidating them and crushing them completely.

If your Crushing is weak, they will be able to rally. The heart of this is to grasp what you have in hand and crush them. You should understand this thoroughly.

Again, when you are in one-on-one martial arts situations, if your opponent is inferior to you, or his rhythm has broken, or if he appears as though he is going to retreat, it is essential that you crush him immediately, without letting him catch his breath or even letting him glance at you. It is your primary consideration to not let him recover even a little. You should investigate this thoroughly.

MOUNTAINS AND SEAS

The heart of Mountains and Seas is that it is wrong to use the same tactic repeatedly during a fight between you and your opponent. Using the same tactic twice is unavoidable, but you should not use it three times. If you use a technique on your opponent and it is not successful the first time, it will have no effect to attack him once more with the same move.

Attack suddenly with a different technique, and if that has no effect, you should use yet a different one. Thus, if your opponent is thinking "mountains," attack with "seas"; and if he is thinking "seas," attack with "mountains." This is the heart of the Way of the Martial Arts. You should investigate this thoroughly.

PIERCING THE BOTTOM

In fighting your opponent and using the principles of this Way, there may be times when you appear to be winning on the surface, but hostility remains in your opponent's mind. Accordingly, he may be defeated on the surface but not at all in the bottom of his mind. In such situations, it is important that you suddenly adjust your own mind, destroy your opponent's spirit and make sure that he has been defeated in the very bottom of his heart.

This Piercing the Bottom can be done with the sword, the body or the mind. It cannot be defined sweepingly.

When your opponent has collapsed from the bottom of his

heart, it is not necessary for you to remain intent; but if he has not, you must remain alert. It will be difficult for your opponent to collapse completely if something remains in his mind.

For the martial arts of both large numbers and one-on-one, you should practice Piercing the Bottom thoroughly.

RENEWAL

When you and your opponent are fighting and nothing is going right, nor is there progress, be of a mind to throw off your former intention and start entirely anew. Take on another rhythm and see your way to victory. With Renewal, whenever you think that you and your opponent are just grating along, you should change your mind on the spot and take the victory by using another tactic.

In martial arts involving large numbers, as well, it is essential to discern a point of Renewal. It is a matter of using your strength of knowledge of the martial arts and seeing through things immediately. You should investigate this thoroughly.

HEAD OF A RAT, NECK OF A BULL

Head of a Rat, Neck of a Bull applies when you are in battle with your opponent and you are both entangled in concentrating on the finer details, yet you feel that you are going nowhere.[3] In the Way of the Martial Arts, you must consider Head of a Rat, Neck of a Bull constantly and repeatedly. No matter how engrossed in the details you are, you should suddenly show great heart and exchange the great and the small. This is one of the dispositions of the martial arts.

It is essential for the warrior, even the ordinary soldier, to think in these terms. You should never depart from this mentality, whether in martial arts involving great numbers or in those of one-on-one. You should investigate this thoroughly.

THE GENERAL KNOWS THE SOLDIERS

In order to fulfill your intentions, and regardless of what kind of fight you may be involved in, you must always put into practice the rule The General Knows the Soldiers. Grasp your strength of wisdom of the martial arts and consider your opponents as your own soldiers. Accordingly, you should make them follow your own intentions and move them around freely. When you think in these terms, you become the general and your opponents become your soldiers. You should make efforts in this.

RELEASING THE HILT OF THE SWORD

There are various meanings to Releasing the Hilt of the Sword. There is the understanding of winning without a sword and the understanding of not winning though you have a sword. There are various meanings, but I will not write them all down. You should practice this thoroughly.

THE BODY OF A ROCKY CRAG

The Body of a Rocky Crag refers to how, grasping the Way of the Martial Arts, you suddenly become like a rocky crag, unmoving and struck by nothing. This is an oral tradition.

The above is what I have written concerning my own style of swordsmanship and is something I have thought over unceasingly. I have written these principles down for the first time, so the order in which they are noted is confused and it is difficult to discuss them in detail. Nevertheless, they should become mental signposts for the person who would study this Way.

From the time I was young I have set my mind on the Way of the Martial Arts, practiced the one subject of swordsmanship with my entire being and experienced various and different understandings. Looking into other styles, I have found that they were either speaking with clever pretexts or demonstrating detailed hand maneuvers; while they looked good to the eye, none of them had the heart of truth.

Of course, you may think it good to learn such things and to practice them with both body and mind. But they all become injurious to the Way and will be impossible to wipe away even in distant generations. Accordingly, they will corrupt the true Way of the Martial Arts in the world and will be the cause of its abandonment.

The true Way of swordsmanship is to fight with your opponent and win, and this should not be changed in the slightest. If you grasp the strength of wisdom of my martial arts and put it directly into practice, there should be no doubt of victory.

Twelfth Day of the Fifth Month, Second Year of Shoho
Shinmen Musashi

THE WIND
CHAPTER

In the martial arts, you know the Way of other styles. As I write about these other styles of martial arts here, I have designated this as "The Wind Chapter."

It would be quite difficult to understand the Way of my style without knowing the Way of others. When you inquire into the other martial arts, you see that there are styles that base their techniques on grasping a large long sword and specializing in strength. There are others that use a small long sword (that is, a short long sword), and exert themselves in their Way. There are yet others who make contrivances with many sword techniques and teach their Way by stances with the sword, saying, "These are the outer stances; these are the inner."[1]

In this chapter, I will express with certainty that none of these are the True Way and will show you what is good, what is bad; what is based on principle and what is not.

The rationale of my own school is completely different. The other schools get along with this as a performance art, as a method of making a living, as a colorful decoration or as a means of forcing flowers to bloom. Yet, can it be the true Way if it has been made into a saleable item? Moreover, the other martial arts in the world only give fine attention to swordsmanship: teaching ways of handling the sword, body postures or hand positions. Can you understand how to win by these things? None of them are the unfailing Way.

In this chapter, I will write down the deficiencies of the other styles one by one. Investigating this thoroughly, you should understand the advantages of the Two-Sword Style.

CARRYING A LONG SWORD IN OTHER STYLES

There are other styles that prefer a long sword.[2] From the standpoint of my own martial art, this can be seen as a weak style. The reason is this: not knowing how to defeat others in any situation, they put virtue in the length of the sword and think they can win by their distance from their opponent. For this reason they prefer a long sword.

The common saying, "A hand longer by an inch has the advantage," is but information quoted by those who do not know the martial arts. Without knowing the principles of the martial arts, they would win at a distance by using a longer sword. Because of their weak hearts, this can be seen as a weak martial art.

When your opponent rushes in close, the longer your sword, the less efficient it becomes. Accordingly, you will be unable to handle your sword freely, it becoming only so much baggage, and you will be at a disadvantage to a man brandishing a small short sword.

Those who prefer long swords will have their explanation, but it is only their own individual quibbling. It is unreasonable when seen from the True Way in this world.

Would you be sure to lose if you did not carry a long sword, but carried a short one instead? Or, according to the situation, what if you were in a place closed in at the top, bottom and sides? Likewise, if you were intent on preferring length and had only a short sword, you might come to doubt your martial art and enter a bad frame of mind.

Depending on the person, there may be those with less strength.[3] Yet, it has been said since ancient times that the large goes together with the small. This is then not a matter of disliking the long unreasonably, but a matter of disliking the mind that prefers the long.

A long sword is like having many men in martial arts situations involving large numbers, while a short sword is like having few men. Do large and small forces not meet in battle? There are many examples of small forces defeating large ones.

In my martial art, we dislike such one-sidedness and narrowness of mind. You should investigate this thoroughly.

USING THE SWORD FORCEFULLY IN OTHER STYLES

There should be no such thing as forceful or weak strokes with the sword. The sword handled with a forceful frame of mind is going to be rough, and it is difficult to win with roughness alone. Moreover, when you go to cut someone forcefully with your sword, you will try to cut with unreasonable strength, and this will not be the right mentality for cutting at all. It is wrong to cut with great strength even when you are testing your blade.

When you cross swords with an opponent, no matter who

he is, do not think about cutting forcefully or weakly. Simply, when you consider cutting someone down, do not use a forceful frame of mind. Nor, of course, a weak one. Think only so far as your opponent's dying.

If both you and your opponent strike forcefully with your swords, the strain will be too much and the result undoubtedly bad. And, if you hit someone's sword forcefully, your own sword will probably break as well. Therefore, do not use your sword forcefully.

Even in martial arts situations involving large numbers, if you are thinking of going into battle with a strong number of men, your opponent will likely be thinking of doing the same. Accordingly, both sides will be equal. In my style, you do not think about overdoing anything in the least. Be intent on winning in any situation by your strength of knowledge of the martial arts. You should make thorough efforts in this.

USING THE SHORT SWORD IN OTHER STYLES

To think that you will win using only a short sword is not the True Way. Since times past, the terms long sword (太刀) and sword (刀) have been used to express how long or short a blade is.[4] In this world, people of great strength are able to easily handle a long sword, and so there is no need for them to unreasonably prefer a short one. Accordingly, for the sake of length you carry a spear or a long long sword. With short long swords, people think they can thread their way through the gaps of others flailing regular swords, dash into their midst and lay hold of their opponents. But this is one-sided thinking and wrong.

Moreover, aiming at unguarded moments can be considered the same as being constantly on the defensive. This is undesirable because your mind becomes entangled. It will be useless in the middle of a large number of opponents to take a short sword and rush into their midst hoping to take a trophy. Some may think they can use a short sword to cut their way into a large crowd, leaping and moving around, but they will always be on the defensive and entangled. This is not the sure Way. All things being the same, mine is a Way in which it is important that you attack vigorously and directly, chasing your opponents around, making them jump back and confusing them and gaining the victory with certainty.

This principle applies, as well, in martial arts situations involving large numbers. All things being the same, it is an essential point of the martial arts that you are intent on rushing into your opponents quickly with a large number of men and crushing those opponents immediately.

When people in this world study these things, they ordinarily learn parrying, dodging, withdrawing and evading. But these draw their minds from the Way and allow them to be pushed around by others. Because the Way of the Martial Arts is direct and true, it is essential that you be intent on pursuing others and subjugating them with true principles. You should investigate this thoroughly.

USING MANY TECHNIQUES WITH THE SWORD IN OTHER STYLES

Teaching people many techniques with the sword makes the Way into a saleable item, and the knowledge of many sword techniques is for the sake of impressing the beginner. This is undesirable in the martial arts. The reason for this is that thinking of the various different ways of cutting someone down confuses the mind.

In this world, there are no extraordinary ways of cutting someone down. For those who know, for those who don't know, for women and children as well, there are not many ways to strike, beat or cut. Other than the method of "cutting down," there are only those of stabbing and slicing. Since this is, first of all, a way of cutting a person down, there are not so many fine details.

Nevertheless, according to the place and condition—as in being cramped in from above and at the sides—you can carry a sword without using it. There are fives ways of doing this, and they are called the Five Directions. Otherwise, cutting people down by additionally twisting your hand, contorting your body, jumping or opening up is not the True Way. Cutting someone down cannot be done by twisting, contorting, leaping or opening up. Such things are absolutely useless.

In my martial art, it is essential that both body and mind are composed in a straightforward way, and that you bend and warp your *opponent*, taking the victory by twisting and distorting your opponent's mind. You should investigate this thoroughly.

USING OTHER STANCES WITH THE SWORD

It is harmful to specialize in stances with the sword. In this world, taking stances should be done when there is no opponent present. The reason for this is that, in examples from the past and practices from today, establishing hard and fast rules is not the Way of victory. That (Way) is in devising difficulties for your opponent.

In all things, the heart of taking a stance is in not being moved. The idea of taking a stance at a castle in battle array, for example, is that you stand strongly unmoved even though you are attacked. This is normal.

In the Way of victory through the Martial Arts, you are intent on taking the initiative—always the initiative—in all things. The heart of taking a stance is in waiting for the initiative. You should make thorough efforts in this.

In the Way of victory through the Martial Arts, you move the other person's stance: you do something your opponent is not expecting, fluster him, make him uncomfortable, threaten him or grasp the rhythm of his confusion. If you seize the victory in these ways, taking a stance will be understood as taking the defensive, and this will be undesirable.

Accordingly, my own Way is that of Stance-No-Stance, which is to say, taking a stance by having no stance at all.

In martial arts situations involving large numbers, it is important for the battle that you consider the number of your opponents' troops, understand the condition of the battlefield, know the abilities of your own men and, grasping the virtues of these things, set up your men and start the fight. What doubles the chances of winning or losing is whether the other side takes the initiative or you yourself take the initiative.

To think that you will take up a fine stance with the sword, adroitly parry your opponent's sword and then strike him well is the same as using spears and long swords as boards in a palisade. Again, the crux of this is that when you strike your opponent, you can pull up a board from a palisade and use it as a spear or long sword. You should investigate this thoroughly.

FIXING THE EYES IN OTHER STYLES

How to fix the eyes goes according to the style. Some fix their eyes on their opponent's sword, while in other styles they fix their eyes on their opponent's hands. Others fix their eyes on the face, and others on the feet. All of these, as they fix their eyes on one special place, confuse the mind and pose a malady to the martial arts.

This is the reason. Although those who play *kemari* do not fix their eyes on the ball, they are able to execute the difficult techniques of the game.[5] Because they have become accustomed to it, it is not a matter of a certain place to look. For the techniques of people doing acrobatic tricks, each becomes accustomed to their Way, whether it be balancing a sliding door on the nose or juggling a number of swords. For such things as these, though they do not fix their eyes in one certain place, it looks natural because they have practiced habitually.

In the Way of the Martial Arts as well, by becoming used to fighting with different opponents, by learning the proportions of a man's mind and by grasping the practice of the Way, you will be able to see through the distance and speed of his sword. Fixing the eyes in the martial arts is looking into the large picture of a man's mind.

In martial arts situations involving large numbers, set your eyes on the abilities and conditions of your opponents' men.

Of the two ways of observation and seeing, the eye of observation is the strongest. It is essential that you take the victory straightaway by seeing the mind of your opponent and the conditions of the place, by fixing your eyes broadly and by see-ing the condition of the battlefield and its different possible strengths and weaknesses.

In the martial arts of both large numbers and one-on-one, do not fix the eye with a narrow focus. As mentioned before, if you fix the eye with a detailed, narrow focus, you will miss the large picture, create for yourself a confused mind and be stripped of a sure victory. You should investigate these principles thor-oughly and put them into practice.

USE OF THE FEET IN OTHER STYLES

In the use of the feet, there are various quick ways of step-ping, called things like Floating Feet, Leaping Feet, Spring-ing Feet, Stamping Feet or Crow's Feet. From the viewpoint of my own martial art, I think them all to be insufficient.[6]

Floating Feet is undesirable because when engaged in a fight, your feet will very likely have a tendency to feel loose. Accord-ingly, my Way is to step with all the more stability. As for the undesirability of Leaping Feet, when you leap up using this step, your mind will become absorbed in the action of leaping. And, as there is no reason for you to leap up many times anyway, Leaping Feet is wrong. As for Springing Feet, again, if your mind is set on springing, it will go no farther than this. Stamping Feet, as a step of waiting, is particularly undesirable. Other than these, there are various other quick steps like the Crow's Feet.

You may cross swords with an opponent in swamps, damp land, mountains, rivers, pebbled plains or narrow roads; depending on the place, there may be no leaping or springing, and there will be places where you will not be able to take quick steps at all.

There is no change in your steps in my martial art. It is like your usual walking on a road. Following your opponent's rhythm, you should grasp the conditions and abilities of his body, both when he is hurried and when he is at ease, and then move, neither insufficiently nor too much, without stepping over yourself.

Managing your steps is essential, as well, in martial arts situations involving large numbers. Here is the reason: when you attack quickly and indiscriminately, without knowing the mind of your opponent, you will confuse your own rhythm and make it difficult to gain the victory.

Moreover, if your steps are too slow, you will not detect the moment when your opponent may be flustered and fall apart; victory will escape you, and you will be unable to win quickly.

It is essential to take the victory by seeing through to the place of your opponent's confusion and collapse, and by not giving him a moment to collect himself. You should practice this thoroughly.

USING SPEED IN OTHER STYLES

Speed in the martial arts is not the True Way. Concerning speed, we say that something is fast or slow depending on whether it misses the rhythm of things.

If someone is skilled in this Way, he does not appear to be fast. For example, if someone is said to be fast on the road, he may cover a distance of forty or fifty *ri*, yet this is not a matter of running fast from morning till night. A man unskilled on the road may run all day long, but will not make much progress.

In the dance of Noh drama, if a skilled person is chanting and an unskilled person accompanies him, the latter will feel as though he is falling behind and will then become hurried. Also, in the play *Oimatsu*, the beat for both small and large drums is tranquil, but an unskilled player will feel behind or ahead of the beat in turn. In the play *Takasago*, the beat is quick, but it is wrong to go too fast. "Run fast and you'll fall down," warns against missing the beat.

Of course, being slow is also wrong. Here, too, a skillful person may appear slow, but he is never off the beat. No matter what a well-trained person does, he never appears hurried.

With these examples, you should understand the principles of the Way.

In the Way of the Martial Arts, particularly, it is bad to go fast. The reason for this is that, according to the place—there may be swamps or damp areas—it may be difficult for either body or feet to go fast. It will be all the more impossible to cut someone down quickly with your sword. If you try to cut him down quickly, it will not be done as if using a fan or a short sword. Accordingly, if you make to cut quickly, you will not cut at all. You should understand this thoroughly.

In martial arts situations involving large numbers, it is wrong to have a mentality of "fast" or "slow." With the mind of Pressing Down the Pillow, you will not go slowly at all. Again, if someone is indiscriminately fast, it is essential that you counter this, become tranquil yourself and not be pulled into this speed by him. You should make efforts and practice the meaning of this.

INTERIOR AND EXTERIOR IN OTHER STYLES

In the martial arts, what is meant by "exterior" and what is meant by "interior"? According to the art or what you touch upon, these terms speak of esoteric meanings and secret traditions as well as entrances to the "interior." But when it comes to the principles of crossing swords with your opponent, there is no such thing as fighting by means of the "exterior" and cutting someone down by means of the "interior."

My way of teaching the martial arts is to take a man who is a beginner in the Way; have him learn according to those skills that he may develop well; teach him principles that he will quickly understand first; see through the places where his mind may be suitable for matters not easily understood; and gradually, gradually, teach him the deeper principles later.

Nevertheless, this is a matter of having him learn how to cross swords in battle, so there is no point called "the entrance to the interior."

In this world, then, when searching for the interior or depths of a mountain, if you think of going even farther into the interior than you already are, you will go right out of the entrance again. In the Way of any subject at all, there are points fitting for the interior and good things regarding coming through the entrance. Here, concerning the principles of battle, what should be hidden? What exposed?

Accordingly, in teaching my Way, I dislike such things as written oaths or contracts with retribution.

Observing the strength of knowledge of the person studying this Way, I teach him what is correct, have him discard the failings of the various other styles of the martial arts and direct him naturally into the True Way of the practices of a warrior with no doubts in his mind. This is my way of teaching the martial arts. You should practice this thoroughly.

In the above nine sections of "The Wind Chapter," I have written an outline of the other styles of the martial arts. Although it is necessary to write down with certainty about the various styles from their entrances to their depths, I have purposely not recorded either the names of those styles or the names of their greatest concerns.

The reason for this is that the view of each style and the explanations of each Way go according to the mentalities of different people. Thus, there are some differences of opinion within the same style. Accordingly, for the sake of those in the future, I have not written about the course of each style.

Throughout the nine sections of general explanations about the other styles, when shown from the correct human reasoning, the various Ways in this world favor long swords or find benefit in short swords alone. But to be predisposed toward strength or weakness in rough terms or in detail are all partial ways. Accordingly, though I have not revealed the entrances and depths of other styles, all should understand this.

In my style, there is neither entrance nor depth to the sword, and there is no ultimate stance. There is only seeing through to its virtues with the mind. This is the essence of the martial arts.

Twelfth Day of the Fifth Month, Second Year of Shoho
Shinmen Musashi

THE EMPTINESS
CHAPTER

It is in "The Emptiness Chapter" that I write down the Way of the Martial Arts of the Two-Sword Style.

The heart of Emptiness is in the absence of anything with form and the inability to have knowledge thereof.[1] This I see as Emptiness. Emptiness, of course, is nothingness. Knowing the existent, you know the nonexistent. This, exactly, is Emptiness. To be in the world and see things poorly, to be unable to distinguish one matter from another and to regard this as Emptiness—this is not the true Emptiness. All that is just the mind of confusion.

When you are on the Way of the Martial Arts, you may perform this Way as a warrior, but if you are ignorant of the warrior's practices, you will not abide in Emptiness. You will be confused and will not do the things that you should. Though you term this "Emptiness," it will not be the true Emptiness.

A warrior learns the Way of the Martial Arts with certainty, makes strong efforts in other martial accomplishments and is not the least bit in the dark about the Way of conducting himself as a warrior. He has no confusion in his mind and is never lazy at any moment of the day. He polishes the two hearts of his mind and will, and sharpens the two eyes of broad observation and focused vision. He is not the least bit clouded, but rather clears away the clouds of confusion. You should know that this is true Emptiness.

While you are yet ignorant of true Emptiness, you may think through your own certain Way, relying on neither Buddhism nor the laws of society, and think this is good. But when you see things from the straight Way of the mind, taking in the world at large, you will see that each person will have the preferences of his own heart, and each eye will have its own distortions. This is turning your back on the True Way.

Know the meaning of this, and make the straightforward your foundation. Make the heart of truth your Way, practice a broad spectrum of the martial arts and understand the expansive correctly and clearly. Accordingly, you will make Emptiness the Way, and see the Way as Emptiness.

Bodhidharma Crossing the Yangtze River on the Branch of a Ditch Reed by Miyamoto Musashi

In Emptiness exists Good but no Evil.

Wisdom is Existence.

Principle is Existence.

The Way is Existence.

The Mind is Emptiness.

Twelfth Day of the Fifth Month, Second Year of Shoho

Shinmen Musashi

NOTES

INTRODUCTION

1. Harima is in present-day Hyogo Prefecture, Mimasaka in Okayama Prefecture.

2. Takuan Soho, *The Unfettered Mind*.

3. The Buddhist manifestation of compassion.

4. Or Buddhas. Often, there is no generic plural for Japanese nouns.

5. Another name for Kannon.

THE EARTH CHAPTER

1. This is literally "Two Heavens, One Current" (二天一流), the last character being used for both "current" and "style." It is also used to denote a "school" for the various arts in Japan.

2. Kannon, or Avalokitesvara, is the bodhisattva of mercy in Buddhism. Also called Kanzeon.

3. That is, 文武二道 (*bunbu nidō*), literally "culture (or literature) and

the martial, two Ways." This is the ancient Confucian ideal and was the Japanese ideal for the warrior since Heian times. A warrior was expected to have both literary and martial skills.

4. Much as we speak of the House of Windsor or the House of Tudor.

5. These are swords of two different lengths. In the first pair, the *tachi* (太刀) is a long sword, and the *katana* (刀) is short. As times changed, the long sword became known as the *katana*, while the short sword was called a *wakizashi* (脇差). Musashi generally uses the term *tachi* for long sword, but for convenience I will call this simply "a sword." A *wakizashi* will be called a short sword unless there is some special designation being given in the text itself.

6. The word here translated as "martial arts," *heiho* (兵法), presents a problem. The first character, 兵, can mean variously "soldier," "warfare," "arms," or "strategy." The original Chinese character seems to have indicated an ax in each hand, and thus "a man wielding weapons." To define it here as "martial" is, then, quite appropriate. The second character, 法, is a little more complicated. It can mean variously "law," "method," "technique," "art," "model," "system" or "doctrine," and originally seemed to have meant something that would dam up or regulate water. In Buddhism, with which Musashi was well versed, it could mean the Truth, phenomenon or the very practice of Buddhism. Though there exists the word *gei* (芸), used to categorize other arts, such as the Tea Ceremony, Noh recitation or archery, Musashi pointedly uses it quite sparingly to describe his "Way." Nevertheless, to use words such as "law", "science" or even "technique" seems to miss the point and to repudiate a practice of modern parlance. I will use the term "martial art," but the reader should keep the other definitions in mind.

7. 1 *ken* = 6 feet.

8. The text actually says, "Their advantages will be many," but most commentators think this is a misprint, as the context would indicate.

THE WATER CHAPTER

1. These two terms, observation (観) and seeing (見), need some explanation. What I have defined as "observation" here can also include the meanings of "contemplation" or "looking through." Zen Buddhists use the term *kanshin* (観心) to mean "meditating on the mind," or "looking through to your true essence," and the term *kannen* (観念) to mean "meditation" or "contemplation." Thus it is to "see" broadly and with introspection. "Seeing" (見) has a more physical sense to it, and the character originally depicted an eyeball with running legs to show, perhaps, the action of physical sight. Musashi uses these two to draw a distinction, and the reader should not depend on the surface meanings of the two English words.

2. That is, not to be distracted by it.

3. Here Musashi uses the word *katana* (刀), but he is writing generally about the long sword, or *tachi* (太刀).

4. Literally, the Two-Waisted Rhythm. The waist (腰) is often found in idioms having to do with working, taking a stand or performing some function.

5. *Shuko*, called either the Autumn Monkey (秋猿) or the Grieving Monkey (愁猿), is employed by Musashi because of its reputed short arms.

6. The term here is "short long sword" (短き太刀).

7. That is, lower the tip of the sword.

8. Although these words literally mean "shout" and "cry," respectively, they were imported from the Chinese and used individually as exclamations. *Katsu*, in particular, was used by Zen priests (with whom Musashi was familiar) to help break through their students' mental barriers. Although there is much shouting in *kendo* and in Japanese martial arts in general, here the words seem to indicate a rhythm more than an actual exclamation.

9. 1 *ri* = 2.44 miles.

THE FIRE CHAPTER

1. The word *kage* can mean either "shadow" or "light." Although in the titles of this and the preceding section, *kage* is written in the *kana* syllabary (かげ), which could denote either meaning, they are distinguished by Chinese characters in their first sentences: 陰, or "shadow," in the preceding section; 影, or "light," in this section. Japanese commentators point out that the former *kage* cannot be seen, while the latter can.

2. See "The Emptiness Chapter."

3. Head of a Rat, Neck of a Bull is a common military saying in Japan. It means that you must be both clever and have great courage. Lacking either one of the two may be disastrous.

THE WIND CHAPTER

1. That is, the beginning stances and the more sophisticated ones.

2. This is literally "a large long sword (大きなる太刀)," but for the sake
   of smoothness, it will be translated simply as "a long sword," with
   "sword" being understood as a *tachi*, or "long sword."

3. Possibly a misprint for "those who use short swords."

4. Generally, the long sword (太刀) is 3 feet or more; the sword (刀) is
   from 2 to 3 feet; and the short sword (脇差), about 1 foot 8 inches.
   Again, except for a very few places, Musashi uses the term *tachi*, or
   long sword, almost exclusively, and this has been translated as
   "sword."

5. *Kemari* was a sort of ceremonial kickball played among the aristoc-
   racy.

6. Musashi uses an untranslatable pun here. "Insufficient" is written
   with the Chinese characters 不足, or "not feet," so that he might
   be saying that all of these feet are really no feet at all.

THE EMPTINESS CHAPTER

1. Despite this first sentence, Musashi's Emptiness would seem to be

the Emptiness of Mahayana Buddhism. The core of the *Heart Sutra*, with which Musashi was undoubtedly acquainted, states that "Form is no other than Emptiness, Emptiness no other than Form; Form is exactly Emptiness, Emptiness exactly Form."

BIBLIOGRAPHY

PRIMARY SOURCES

Miyamoto Musashi. *Gorin no sho*. Annotated by Nakamura Naokatsu. Tokyo: Kodansha, 1970.

Miyamoto Musashi. *Gorin no sho*. Annotated by Watanabe Ichiro. Tokyo: Iwanami Shoten, 1985.

Miyamoto Musashi. *Gorin no sho*. Translation into modern Japanese by Kamata Shigeo. Tokyo: Kodansha, 1986.

SECONDARY SOURCES

Awakawa Yasuichi. *Zen Painting*. Tokyo: Kodansha International, Ltd., 1970.

Fischer, Felice. *The Arts of Hon'ami Koetsu, Japanese Renaissance Master*. Philadelphia: Philadelphia Museum of Art, 2000.

Hakeda Yoshito. *Kukai: Major Works*. New York: Columbia University Press, 1972.

Leach, Bernard. *Kenzan and His Tradition*. New York: Transatlantic Arts, Inc.,1967.

Lubarsky, Jared. *Noble Heritage: Five Centuries of Portraits from the Hosokawa Family*. Washington, D.C.: Smithsonian Institution, 1992.

Takuan Soho. *The Unfettered Mind*. Translation by William Scott Wilson. Tokyo: Kodansha International, Ltd., 1986.

CREST MOTIFS

The traditional Japanese crest remains an intriguing element of Japanese design even today. In older times, beginning around the end of the twelfth century, popular motifs were adopted as stylized symbols by individuals, groups, or families, often as heraldic emblems of a military faction or clan. Later, when peace settled over the country, crests evolved further and their usage became fashionable for clothing. Contemporary personalities, tradesmen and commercial enterprises adopted crests as emblems. The crests in this volume are shown here with their basic pattern names. The larger looped pattern at the beginning of the foreword and introduction is a silhouette of a sword guard (*tsuba*) from Musashi's age.

BALANCE WEIGHT

ENCIRCLED
BAMBOO

IRIS IN
STREAM

FOUR SWORDS
AND WOOD
SORREL

FLOWER IN
TORTOISE SHELL

HANGING
WISTERIA

CRESCENT MOON
AND
NORTH STAR

MOKKO

SINGLE EDDIED
WAVE

SIX SWORDS
ENCIRCLED

ENCIRCLED
SPATTERDOCK
LEAF

SIX-SICKLE
WHEEL

THREE DRAWER
PULLS

(英文版) 五輪書
The Book of Five Rings

2002年 1 月　第 1 刷発行
2008年 5 月　第14刷発行

著　者　　宮本武蔵
英　訳　　ウィリアム・スコット・ウィルソン
発行者　　富田 充
発行所　　講談社インターナショナル株式会社
　　　　　〒112-8652 東京都文京区音羽 1-17-14
　　　　　電話　03-3944-6493 （編集部）
　　　　　　　　03-3944-6492 （営業部・業務部）
　　　　　ホームページ　www.kodansha-intl.com
印刷・製本所　大日本印刷株式会社

© ウィリアム・スコット・ウィルソン 2002
Printed in Japan
ISBN 978-4-7700-2801-3